Directing the Sitcom

Directing the Sitcom
Joel Zwick's Steps for Success

JOEL ZWICK *and*
ROSARIO J. ROVETO, JR.

Foreword by Tom Hanks

McFarland & Company, Inc., Publishers
Jefferson, North Carolina

All illustrations in Step 8 are by Wes Simpkins.

LIBRARY OF CONGRESS CATALOGUING-IN-PUBLICATION DATA

Names: Zwick, Joel, author. | Roveto, Rosario J., Jr., author.
Title: Directing the sitcom : Joel Zwick's steps for success / Joel Zwick and Rosario J. Roveto, Jr. ; foreword by Tom Hanks.
Description: Jefferson, North Carolina : McFarland & Company, Inc., Publishers, 2016 | Includes bibliographical references and index.
Identifiers: LCCN 2016032515 | ISBN 9781476665566 (softcover : acid free paper) ∞
Subjects: LCSH: Situation comedies (Television programs)— Production and direction—United States. | Television— Production and direction—United States.
Classification: LCC PN1992.8.C66 Z85 2016 | DDC 791.4502/33—dc23
LC record available at https://lccn.loc.gov/2016032515

BRITISH LIBRARY CATALOGUING DATA ARE AVAILABLE

ISBN (print) 978-1-4766-6556-6
ISBN (ebook) 978-1-4766-2517-1

© 2016 Joel Zwick and Rosario J. Roveto, Jr. All rights reserved

No part of this book may be reproduced or transmitted in any form or by any means, electronic or mechanical, including photocopying or recording, or by any information storage and retrieval system, without permission in writing from the publisher.

Front cover: Joel Zwick on the set of *Girl Meets World*, 2015; background © 2016 iStock

Printed in the United States of America

*McFarland & Company, Inc., Publishers
Box 611, Jefferson, North Carolina 28640
www.mcfarlandpub.com*

To all the many artists, craft persons, grips, electricians, painters, script supervisors, dialogue coaches, writers, producers, actors, dancers, choreographers and assistant directors that I have had the great luck to have worked with these almost 40 years. This book would not have been possible without you.

To my close friends (I hope you know who you are), thanks for all your support.

To Candice, my loving wife, our children, Lara, Jodi, Jamie and Hillary, our son-in-laws, Phillip and Jermaine, our grandkids, Elliott, Olive and Aubrey, thanks for all you do. I love you.—*Joel Zwick*

To Christine and Rosario, Sr. (Mom and Dad), who always supported my career by giving me the freedom to continually expand my imagination from my childhood into adulthood. My brothers James and Arthur, who helped shape the person I am today. Frank Pace, who mentored me throughout the years, and Joel and Diane Steiger, who enabled me to continue my pursuit of a career in Hollywood with their hospitable generosity. However, most of all my daughter, Tatiana, my biggest inspiration and supporter. She has unselfishly endured my time away and continues to impress me with her spirit, her love and her own vivid imagination that keeps our creative star shining bright!—*Rosario J. Roveto, Jr.*

TABLE OF CONTENTS

Foreword by Tom Hanks   1
Introduction by Rosario J. Roveto, Jr.   3

Joel's Approach to the Sitcom   9

Step 1: Preparation
Day 1: Meetings and Rehearsal   28
Production Meeting: Prep and Execution   28
Mechanics of the Production Meeting and Making Decisions   29
Special Equipment   34
Visualization of the Set   35
The Table Read   36
The Pilot: How You Can Help Shape a Show   38
The Table Read for Your First Time Directing a Show   41
Putting It on Its Feet   42
Rehearsal Advice for the First-Timer on a Show   42
Rehearsing Joel's Style and Actor Resistance   43

Step 2: Staging
Day 2: Building a Solid Foundation   47
Staging: Set Notes for Camera and First-Time Advice   47
Staging: Applying the Learned Scene   50
Staging: The Physical Manifestation of the Story   53
Disciplining the Physical Excesses of an Actor   58

Step 3: Dialogue
Day 2: Engaging the Actors   60
The Importance of Dialogue   60
Pacing and Cues and Acting Styles   62
Rules of Comedy and Directing Actors   64
But I Didn't Study Acting ...   67
Sense of Humor   68

TABLE OF CONTENTS

Step 4: Fine Tuning the Acting
    Day 2: The Tools of the Craft   69
    Time Management   69
    The Importance of Props   70
    Lines, Movement and Placement   72

Step 5: Writers' and Producers' Run-Through
    Day 2: Final Preparation   75
    Writer-Producer Run-Through   75
    Making Animals and Actors Work   78

Step 6: Applying Producer Notes
    Day 3: How to Improve the Play   82
    Preparing for the Network Run-Through   82

Step 7: Network Run-Through
    Day 3: Performing for the Network   87
    Importance of the Network Run-Through   87

Step 8: Shooting the Show
    Day 4: Preparing for the Shoot   90
    The Shooting Draft and the Technical Crew   90
    Definition of Framing and Composition   91
    Camera Shots and Coverage   98
    The Proscenium and Its Multiples   104
    The Importance of Resets   106
    The Short Wall   111
    Pass Coverage   113
    Conceptualizing the Story with Four Cameras   115
    Commercial Breaks   119
    Traditional Camera Blocking with Stand-Ins   120
    Specialty Shots: Do You or Don't You Reinvent the Show?   121
    Is Shooting Comedy Formulaic?   123

Step 9: Adjusting the Shoot
    Day 4: Accomodating the Network and Producers   128
    Network Notes and the Changing Industry   128

Table of Contents

Step 10: Final Shoot
    Day 5: Performing for a Live Audience   133
    Show Time   133
    The Booth vs. the Floor   139
    The Director's Cut   145

Conclusion
    Making Comedy Fun: The Life of a Sitcom Director   149
    Separating Your Style from the System   156

Glossary   159
Index   169

Foreword by Tom Hanks

Some phone calls you remember for the rest of your life because they change your life. In the spring of 1980 a call came into my dingy Hell's Kitchen railroad flat. Joel Zwick was on the line from California and he had good news.

Joel had been the director of the pilot episode of *Bosom Buddies*—I had won the show-biz lottery and been cast in the sitcom with Peter Scolari, Wendi Jo Sperber, Telma Hopkins, Donna Dixon and the fabulous Holland Taylor. At Paramount Studios, smack in the middle of Hollywood for two weeks the previous March, we had rehearsed and, in one long day of three-camera filming, shot the half-hour show under Joel's wildly energetic direction. He laughed like mad. He approached blocking the actors and the camera moves with an infectious enthusiasm, bouncing on the balls of his sneaker-clad feet, hollering at us things like "Try it! Try it!" or "But I can't *shoot that!*"

Joel already had a long history as a director. In New York he had worked at the famed Off Off Broadway La MaMa Theater. On television his name was on a ton of episodes of *Laverne & Shirley*. He had directed pilot after pilot and there he was in charge of the only job I ever had in TV. It was a good thing Joel was our director, as I had no idea what I was doing.

I met him at the first *Bosom Buddies* read-through, held in a conference room on what had been the RKO movie lot, later the Desilu Studios, and then the home of such hit shows as *Happy Days*, *Mork and Mindy* and *Taxi*. It was a setting so fraught with legendary trappings of Tinseltown that even the HOLLYWOOD sign was visible just up on the hill.

At the conference room table, Joel immediately guided us along. He told us to work on "hooks" (those choices that become the signature bits of our characters), to trust our instincts and to come to work ready to play. It took about 32 minutes to read through that first script—22 minutes for the dialogue with a ten-minute spread due to Joel's laughter. The two weeks of making the show went by in a heady mix of work and more of that time-cheating laughter, resulting in a TV show that was still only a pilot, meaning *Bosom Buddies* might never have been seen on television and my first big job would have lasted exactly two weeks.

But, on that afternoon when my Hell's Kitchen phone rang, Joel Zwick was telling me different: The show had sold and would be on ABC on Thursday nights come the fall of 1980. And life changed.

Then, Joel bailed on *Bosom Buddies*! That rat! For the first of the two seasons we were on the air, Joel Zwick had taken his directing chops to *It's a Living*, a show that also aired on Thursday nights; a show with actual women and not two guys in drag. Was that the attraction to leave us, I wondered?

Some talented directors came and went our first season but by the first episode of the next year, Joel was back at our helm, with the bouncing feet and the big laughs echoing around Paramount Stage 25, where he stayed for all but our final episode (which was directed by the creator and executive producer of *Bosom Buddies* Chris Thompson).

Though the job ended, the friendship did not. Joel and I stayed in contact with constant checking-in and career summit meetings. Years later I was able to convince the powers-that-be that Joel was the perfect director for the film *My Big Fat Greek Wedding*. He would help define the characters, he would tell the story, he would get the shots, and he would be as expert with the comedy as he was quick with the schedule. And he was.

This book will extrapolate on his natural enthusiasm and learned directing chops and be as entertaining as the man himself. If you are in the Business of Show, I suggest you highlight passages and keep notes because Joel just might change your life.

Tom Hanks has won two Academy Awards for Best Actor, seven Emmys and numerous other honors in his career.

Introduction
by Rosario J. Roveto, Jr.

Situation comedy, also called sitcom, radio or television comedy series that involves a continuing cast of characters in a succession of episodes. Often the characters are markedly different types thrown together by circumstance and occupying a shared environment such as an apartment building or workplace. Sitcoms are typically half an hour in length; they are either taped in front of a studio audience or employ canned applause, and they are marked by verbal sparring and rapidly resolved conflicts.... Encyclopædia Britannica.

When I first started working on a new multi-camera Disney series entitled *Shake It Up*, I had the fortunate opportunity of being the show's first assistant director (1AD). My job was to do just that, assist the director. The position calls for applying many managerial skills to help facilitate the production of a television show. I'm not going to get into details but in short, it is a highly respected position with many facets and responsibilities. What I will focus on is how the 1AD has the golden opportunity to watch the director of a multi-camera television series work their craft on a daily basis. It's like going to directing school and getting paid for it!

If you have any kind of desire to become a multi-camera television director, where else are you going to get a better front row seat to watch, listen and absorb what directors do and how they do it?

Unfortunately, not everyone has this golden opportunity at their disposal so this is why I want to share with you conversations, insight and anecdotes from one master director, Joel Zwick. Under his tutelage, many assistant directors have become effective directors in the world of situation comedies.

With over 600 episodes under his belt, Joel's credits range from classics like *Mork & Mindy, Laverne & Shirley, Bosom Buddies, Perfect Strangers, Full House* and *Webster* to the contemporary hit series *Two and a Half Men, Shake*

Introduction by Rosario J. Roveto, Jr.

It Up, Jessie, Girl Meets World and KC Undercover, with many other multi-camera series filling in the gaps. Joel was also the director of the feature film *My Big Fat Greek Wedding*, the highest-grossing romantic comedy ever. Ironically, a feature film I directed, *A Wake in Providence*, was described in a couple of reviews as having pleasant echoes of *My Big Fat Greek Wedding*. It is not a mystery why Joel and I worked well together. I was very fortunate to work with Joel over three years. This enabled me to hone my multi-camera directing skills and successfully apply them to the *Shake It Up & KC Undercover* episodes I directed.

Rosario J. Roveto, Jr. (left), and Joel Zwick.

Introduction by Rosario J. Roveto, Jr.

Watching Joel Zwick is watching a master craftsman at work. His sense of story, staging, blocking actors for multiple cameras and shot selections are at a point of purely being instinctual magic.

Joel's method of simultaneously shooting with four cameras is genius. Multi-camera shooting is very different from shooting a feature film or episodic television series where you shoot an average of five pages per day with one camera, possibly two if the budget allows.

In single camera television shows you usually only shoot one or two frames in one camera set-up. Then you move your camera to the next set-up for different framing and coverage of the actors. It takes longer to shoot the same coverage in a scene this way as opposed to the multi-camera format because you are using only one or two cameras at most in each set-up. You also have more latitude in single camera shows to complete the scenes that you may not get to shoot on any single day of a sitcom, like additional set-ups and coverage because of the extended schedules. Having more time to shoot episodic single camera shows or feature films lends itself to having a more artsy and stylized look.

Thus, being a slower process, single camera projects are considered less stressful, less demanding (time-wise), generally not as complicated (regarding camera set-ups) and more myopic when compared with the same window of time to shoot a sitcom which is an average of 35–45 pages over two days. There is no latitude in sitcoms. You must shoot out the script in the schedule given so you need to be able to master the steps of shooting this medium in order to satisfy the demanding schedule in a quick, efficient and productive manner.

After reading this book, you will have a clear understanding how to direct a multi-camera situation comedy the Joel Zwick way. Eventually, you will build up the speed which television shows demand given the ambitious productions and tight schedules (especially if child actors are involved) while masterfully capturing all the comedy, whether physical or verbal, in this fun and exciting medium.

Joel Zwick: I remember very clearly the first time Rosario came to me with the notion of writing a book about directing sitcoms and that he wished to base his book on conversations with me about directing.

Introduction by Rosario J. Roveto, Jr.

As I gave the project much thought, I realized that it was the perfect opportunity to get a chance to actually verbalize and perhaps understand what I was doing during the 600-plus episodes of multi-camera sitcoms that I have directed. As Rosario and I began our process, he would record me as I blathered on about this and that. Soon things came into focus. Rosario's first draft, his structuring of the book, made great sense; maybe he was on to something. He had always said that there was no book recently written that detailed how sitcoms were done.

Some of this book deals with how a sitcom week is set up. We deal with staging and shooting, interactions with actors, producers and networks and anecdotal tales from shows past. As we continued to distill what the book was about, it became apparent to me that the examination of craft was critical, *but*: The most important point that I wanted to express was that we can all attain the skills necessary to do the job, but it is the uniqueness of each person, his or her strengths, that shape us as directors.

Know yourself as a person and as an artist and have faith in that. You must nourish your uniqueness as you adhere to the necessities of the job.

I hope that this book not only lays out all the information you will need to understand and start to practice the craft of directing, and also inspires you to be the best that you can be.

* * *

What follows are two items to get you started in the right direction.

Ten Basic Steps

1. Arrive early to stage on Monday to get familiar with the sets and make final notes in your script for the Production Meeting and Table Read.
2. Stage the actors during rehearsal for best placement in the sets.
3. Position the actors with relation to each other to best express the dialogue.
4. Fine-tune the positions of the actors for ease of shooting.
5. Perform a Producer's Run-through on Tuesday, showing the

writers and producers how you have put the Blue Revised Table Draft on its feet.

6. Apply the notes given by the producers to the Wednesday rehearsal process and incorporate any changes in the Pink Revised Table Draft.
7. Perform a Network Run-through to show the network executives and the producers the current state of the play.
8. Understand and execute the shooting process for Thursday and Friday.
9. Shoot and satisfy the network's final notes during pre-shoots.
10. Shoot the Audience Show.

Sample Weekly Schedule

Monday

8:00 a.m.–9:00 a.m.	Production Meeting
9:00 a.m.–10:00 a.m.	Table Read (Table Draft), notes
10:00 a.m.–12:00 p.m.	Rehearsal on Stage
12:00 p.m.–1:00 p.m.	Lunch
1:00 p.m.–3:00 p.m.	Rehearsal on Stage

Tuesday

8:00 a.m.–12:00 p.m.	Rehearsal (Blue Revised Table Draft), Stage
12:00 p.m.–1:00 p.m.	Lunch
1:00 p.m.–3:00 p.m.	Rehearsal
3:00 p.m.–4:30 p.m.	Producers' Run-Through, notes

Wednesday

8:00 a.m.–12:00 p.m.	Rehearsal (Pink Revised Table Draft) on stage
12:00 p.m.–1:00 p.m.	Lunch
1:00 p.m.–3:00 p.m.	Rehearsal
3:00 p.m.–4:30 p.m.	Network Run-Through, notes

Thursday

7:00 a.m.–8:00 a.m.	ESU (Electronic Set-up)
8:00 a.m.–1:00 p.m.	Camera Block and Pre-Shoot (Shooting Draft)
1:00 p.m.–2:00 p.m.	Lunch
2:00 p.m.–TBD	Camera Block and Pre-Shoot

Introduction by Rosario J. Roveto, Jr.

Friday

11:30 a.m.–12:15 p.m.	ESU
12:15 p.m.–3:30 p.m.	Camera Block and Pre-Shoot (Shooting Draft)
3:30 p.m.–4:30 p.m.	Lunch
4:30 p.m.–4:50 p.m.	Cast Speed Read-through with director
4:50 p.m.–5:20 p.m.	Hair and Make-up touch-ups, notes
5:20 p.m.–5:30 p.m.	Cast Intros
5:30 p.m.–TBD	Shoot Audience show

Sidenote: Revision drafts and revision pages are distributed on colored paper, a different color for each set of revisions, with each changed line marked by an asterisk in the right margin of the page. The progression of colors varies from one production to the next, but a typical sequence would be: white, blue, pink, yellow, green, goldenrod, buff, salmon, cherry, tan, ivory, white (this time known as "double white") and back to blue ("double blue").

Joel's Approach to the Sitcom

In this chapter, Joel discusses how he got involved in directing for television. Being lucky enough to get an opportunity isn't enough. It's important to be prepared. Not only prepared to direct actors or handle the technical aspects of the craft but also ready to learn about the psychology of directing. Prepared to deal with all kinds of personalities. Many times it isn't just *mano a mano*, but being challenged to take on many personalities at once. Whether it's the creator of the show, network and studio executives, executive producers, department heads, cast and/or crew, etc., it's essential to understand the system going in and the need to remain confident and strong, while also being receptive. Television is a club. Membership is earned not only by talent but by learning how to develop and maintain relationships.

The System and the Craft

RR *Describe how you felt suited for directing sitcoms and how you first got introduced to the situation comedy.*

JZ Directing a sitcom is a system and you have to find a way to make the system work for you. You may personalize your approach but the system is a given. I have developed a wrinkle on the system that's my own personal style. I've developed a style that's very specific to my energy, to my speed of mind, to my work ethic and to my ability to focus. Those are skill sets that I was born with or grew up with or something that basically made me well-suited to directing sitcoms.

The first time that I saw a sitcom being shot was when I went to see a taping of *Busting Loose,* a show that starred Adam Arkin, in 1978. I went to view an episode while visiting my buddy Greg Antonacci, a star on the show and one of the writers. I was watching this thing thinking to myself, "Well,

Joel's Approach to the Sitcom

this is a piece of cake. They are staging a 25-minute play and they have a whole week to do it." I just finished staging *Oklahoma!* and it had a dream ballet in it that was longer than a sitcom. It seemed to me, "That can't be a hard job. The actors know the characters they are playing and the writers know how to write those characters." I remember when I got my big break, I had been with Greg two weeks and was with him at work when Greg decided that I should direct an episode of *Busting Loose*. I'm thinking, "I'm a person of theater. I don't direct television."

But then I went through a very interesting thinking process. I said, "Wait a minute, big shot. Nobody has asked you to do it. Second of all, you don't know if you can do it. And third of all, you don't know if you'd like doing it." Well, at that point I began to realize that I must take the opportunity. You have to take opportunities and do what has to be done to try to succeed, and then if you still want to return to theater, you can make an informed decision.

So, I had this meeting with Judy Coppage, head of Current Programming with Paramount TV, about directing an episode of *Busting Loose*. I walk into her office and it was the shortest meeting on record. I said, "Listen, I never directed a situation comedy so I am not going to stand here and tell you that I know how to direct sitcoms. But I have been watching for a couple of weeks now and in my estimation, a retarded monkey can direct sitcoms." [*Laughs*] I said to her, "What are they going to do? Are they going to let me point the cameras at each other?" I said that if I can talk to actors and talk to writers, you oughta give me a shot. She looked at me and excused herself for a second. She got on the phone with CBS and said, "I got a guy I'm hiring to direct an episode of *Busting Loose*." I don't know if that's a thing I would tell other directors to try. I think that it was very, very specific to time and place and my Brooklyn chutzpah, but I told her the truth. I believed that the job was that simple. As it turned out, it wasn't that simple, you know. It's the craft that you have to start to develop. It can only develop as you are doing the job and it's very hard to develop craft when you have nothing to experiment with. So, you just have to somehow be good enough to get the first job and be good enough at that first job so they hire you again so you can start to develop craft. As long as you remember that it is the accumulation of craft that will make you successful, you have a good shot. The more craft you got, the better you get. You know, as an AD you've gotten better just because your skill package has matured. Well, it's the same thing for directing. Get out on the floor and your skill package starts to mature and you're finding out that you are seeing camera shots better and you begin to understand how the shooting goes and you understand what your needs are and how you feed the actors. What is it that you think the actors are looking for in the sitcom? Remember, these are professional actors. You are not out there teaching acting. You're out there helping these actors be the best they can be because they've been cast for what it is they do. If they cast a giraffe, make him the best giraffe possible. Do not try to turn him into an elephant.

Political and Social Needs

What is your advice to directors trying to getting a shot in television?
When you get an opportunity, you have to work hard and you have to understand politically what the situation is, what the pecking order is, what you can and can't do in a certain situation. You can't get so full of yourself that somehow you think you can do anything you want because you're the director. Well, this is a very cooperative business. Especially TV. There might be 125 people working on one sitcom in various responsibilities and for the most part you have to be able to hear the needs of all those people if you are the director. You will have to somehow understand that you can't write off people as stupid because they have a Harvard MBA and what do they know about situation comedies? The fact remains that they have a need that has to be answered to and that is the bottom line. You as the director have a severe responsibility that the bottom line is adhered to. That is a political necessity. Then there is the social need. You better be a nice person because we work with nice people. We don't want to work with idiots or fools. All things being equal, we would rather work with people we like. Lastly, you just have to figure out what it is that you do that separates your unique style from what other people do. I figured out from the beginning that if there was any separation for me at all, it was my energy. The word on the *Laverne & Shirley* set was that Cindy Williams ran around the stage screaming at the top of her lungs, "Half my weekly salary to anyone who will put downers in this man's coffee!" [*Laughs*]

So, this has been going on for a long time.
Yeah, for a long time! But, the fact is that Penny [Marshall] and Cindy liked me, because of my New York energy. I had no skills going into *Laverne & Shirley*. I had done the one episode of *Busting Loose*, I came back to New York, directed a play, came back out to California and directed an episode of a Ted Knight show, which was the first show Ted Knight did after *The Mary Tyler Moore Show*. It was a ridiculous premise. The man ran an escort service. What does that mean? [*Laughs*] But nonetheless, I did my episode and eventually Gary Marshall saw some work I did and said he was going to give me a shot with the girls. I had no idea who the girls were at the time. I just thought, "Hey, how cool! I'll get a shot with the girls."

Shaping the System for Speed

How did you make television work for you?
I had to shape the system to how sitcoms were made and to fulfill the needs of a man who is highly energetic. I had to find a way to make speed an asset in how I directed that kept me employed. My mind worked that way anyway, my mind was very fast. My mind could see things quickly, could determine things quickly. I'm not sure where that came from but certainly partly from education and genetics but that was why Penny and Cindy liked having me around. I was fast.

But can that also be learned?
Yes, that can be accessed. It's not unlike an athlete who has skills and spends all his time shooting 10,000 jump shots a day and all of a sudden has a remarkable shot; or someone who has learned to trust his basic craft so that it doesn't even look like he's thinking about what he's going to do and all of a sudden he is doing 360s and dunking the ball when the goal was simply dunking the ball. How the athlete dunks the ball is his style. It's how he works but ultimately the ball got dunked. It's still two points. You don't get extra points for style, nor do you get extra points for style in directing a sitcom. You have to get the job done. "You mean, he can get us out two hours before anybody else and the quality of the work seems to be just as good? What the

hell is this guy doing? How's he doing that?" Well, I'm not doing anything differently than anybody else but my skill package enables me to do it faster and I use that as a goal. I would set goals for myself that nobody else was setting. I determined very early in my career that I was never going to direct with a script. Well, that's a bizarre notion. There are no other directors that don't direct with a script. They were all sitting there with their scripts. I learned the script. Now, I can't tell you the dialogue line by line but I know every joke. I say, "Give me a logline," and all you have to say is, "She eats apple pie" and I got the whole scene. The thing is that I know the scene. I know the movement of the scene. I know how the scene will be shot, I know how the scene looks. I understand the humanity of the scene because I spend a lot of time at night working the script over and over and over and over again until I really understood visually and emotionally the story I am telling. It takes a lot of passes to do that. Now, obviously, 600 episodes in, I can do it much quicker. I can read a script now and virtually stage 90 percent after the first reading and then there is about ten percent of the script where I go, "Hmm, what are they doing there? Well, that's kind of strange. Oh, I see," and it takes me a while to figure out how that should be handled because it's more complicated. It's something that they wrote that's out of the norm that might have to be handled by a huge special effect. You might have a hurricane on stage. You may be setting a fire on stage. You may be flying people doing all kinds of stunt work that requires a different level of inspection that you can't get from reading a script once over. Initially I can't tell you how many times I pored over a script. I would just read it repeatedly until I knew the script and I camera-blocked without a script and I have to tell you that my first episode of *Busting Loose* with Phil Perez as my camera coordinator, I made it through the first three scenes and I was feeling pretty good and then I hit the wall [*laughs*]. I was done. It was over. I looked up at Phil Perez in the stands and said, "Phil, I got nothing else" [*Laughs*], and he just blocked it for me until the end of the day. But I set that goal right from the beginning that I was going to force myself to visualize what it is I thought I should see to tell the story that I thought should be told using the actors that I had to tell that story with. And basically, that was it. I set that goal for myself and because of that today it looks like I'm an instant director. It doesn't look like there is any space between the need and the decision.

Joel's Approach to the Sitcom

Telling the Story First

Directors are storytellers. How did you develop your instincts? You didn't write down the lines of what the cameras were shooting on* Shake It Up. *You were shooting it in your head.

Yes I was. I was visualizing in my head.

You didn't have to write it down?

I did initially.

Tell me about that.

Phil Perez taught me how to mark a script as a director. He taught me how to mark a script so that I understood what the coverage was for each little section of the scene that would need coverage. Phil asked, "What are you shooting there? Is that going to be a two-shot? Because if two people are close together, it is going to have to be a two-shot." "Okay, so that's a two-shot. Now, what happens if I was to separate those two people?" I asked. "If you separate them far enough, you may want to be in singles because at that point the two-shot would be too wide." Phil replied. "Oh, that's interesting. Then why would you want to put them in a two-shot vs. a single or singles?" I asked. "Well, that's a question of story. You think they relate to each other in the same shot or do you think they relate to each other in cuts?" Phil replied. "Oh, okay. Well, that's something to think about." I said. So, therefore the storytelling was a part of figuring out visually how you tell that story. You're trying to visually see the story. I have to find a way to bring those characters together to satisfy the needs of the story. I use an expression called "backstaging" which is a little strange but essentially if I know a moment has to play that's between two people that's warm and sensitive and I have to get those two people together to play that moment, I have to figure out a way in my staging to make sure that they are together by the time that moment is done, otherwise the moment won't be what it needs it to be to tell the story. So, I have to backstage in terms of making sure that before that moment arrives, they are together; and that's what I do throughout a script. Certain scenes are much more complicated but when I talk about the basics, it starts off with simply as, if you have two people on a couch and you have four cameras shooting two people on my couch ... what do you shoot there? What are the options to shoot?

Single Camera vs. Multi-Camera

After the end of *The Cosby Show*, *Seinfeld* and *Friends*, there was a huge dip in people's interest in live-action situation comedy. Essentially, what happened was then, the people who had been basically shadowing, training and trying to learn the intricacies of directing the multi-camera situation comedy shooting were coming out of film school where all their background had been in single camera work. Some of them adapted quite nicely just because of their ability to visualize. But others had a very hard time because of the speed and the necessity of finding out what four cameras are shooting simultaneously as opposed to what one camera is shooting.

That's happening now, too. Directors are either coming in that are not familiar with the multi-camera world and are getting through it technically because of the associate director or camera coordinator; or the flip side where a lot of directors come onto a show and they really don't bring anything to the table regarding the play. They don't create a new dimension with the script in the world of comedy. I just saw it recently. The script could have been bought to a whole different level, and it ...

It never got there.

In the end it's still a writer's medium. They're the ones who are going to bring out the comedy if the director isn't doing it. The thing that would separate a novice director from a good director is the one who can go beyond the technical world and bring added nuances to the play itself.

Essentially, you're quite right. There are two skills that are separate from each other that need to be employed to be a successful situation comedy director. Wherever you come from is not important, it's that you get to the final place because that will be dependent upon how much you tend to work. You have to be able to communicate to actors. You have to have a visionary idea of how comedy plays, and why it's important to have some people in a two-shot and some people have to be in a single. Why it's important that a cross happens here or doesn't happen there. That's a simple way of telling the story.

However, learning how to deploy cameras successfully so that you can shoot this little story that you're being told to shoot without an enormous amount of pain is the next job that you have to learn. If you come with camera experience, you should start to figure out how to talk to actors and learn what acting is about. And if you're an actor-driven director, you better learn the technology of how you manipulate cameras because it's just not fair to expect somebody whose job is not to sit there and camera block a show for you.

What do you think makes the difference between someone like yourself, creating a career in situation comedies, compared to another comedic mastermind, Mel Brooks, who's known for feature films?

I don't think there is. I think there's Mel Brooks. I think that Carl Reiner had a hell of a career, Rob Reiner had a hell of a career. All these people came out of TV although Mel Brooks and Carl Reiner came out of *Your Show of Shows*. They were part of a writing staff that included Woody Allen. My goodness gracious, what a writing staff that had to be. But essentially, no, they found a way to do their comedy in a longer form and I don't know how successful they would have been in multi-camera. I don't know if it's something they would have even cared about doing.

I had an encounter with Mel Brooks that was pretty hysterical. We're doing an episode of *Perfect Strangers* and we're shooting it out on the parking lot of … I think we might have been at Warner Brothers. We had a big house with a big roof. The whole episode was about the guys trying to fix some hole in the roof and it's raining and pouring. There is Mark Linn-Baker and Bronson Pinchot up on this roof and we got this whole thing planned out of what this routine was going to be up there. We were starting to shoot and some guy sidles up to me and says, "It's not going to work." I look over, it's Mel Brooks, and I go, "Yeah?" He says, "Yeah," and walks away. Two weeks later I'm in that parking lot again re-shooting it because it didn't work and sure enough … what are the odds? As I'm re-shooting it, a guy sidles up to me and says, "Told you so," and walks away. That's my great moment of Mel Brooks–isms in my life. He's omnipresent. I have no idea how he showed up both times but I came from New York in a period of time when they thought it was a very good idea to bring in Broadway directors to do situation comedies because it was staging a little 25-minute play. However, some of those guys who turned out to be brilliant in long form never could quite find the energy or the passion for the speed of the multi-camera world. They like to control one shot at a time. They thought they could do better work as a visionary thing.

Jeff Bleckner came out with me and Bleckner and I were good friends. He directed a lot of *Rhoda*s and realized this was not a world he could exist in. He just wasn't fast enough on his feet. He was more ponderous than that but, boy, when he went into mini-series and stuff like that…! He's won multiple Emmy awards. He found his place but he found it through theater to sitcom to long form, which is not a big shock. I mean, sitcom is a great teacher of how scenes and sections of scenes need to be cut. You learn cutting. You're cutting on your feet. You know what can cut together. You're actually a quasi-editor. You can't be shooting things that don't cut together. You have to know how they can cut together and that becomes a skill that you start to gain. If you can survive your youth, you will gain those skills because they're present. They're not difficult to gain.

Bringing Your Style to an Established Show

Even as someone who directed over 500 episodes of television, joining a show like Shake It Up *that was already established, you were basically considered a first-timer. What was your approach?*

On *Shake It Up* I was definitely behaving like a first-timer. I made sure that I got my rear end down to that set and I spent time watching camera blocking. Watching shooting. Watching performance. Watching what these kids in the *Shake It Up* cast were capable of doing. Taking a look at the situation and sizing up how well the system was operating under the director who basically I'm watching.

I figure now that I have to adapt my style to the system. With my experience, I know how I move things but that's not the point. How do I adapt that? How do I adapt that to kids? I had some experience with *Full House* so it wasn't like I'd never directed kids. I'd directed Urkel on *Family Matters*. I've dealt with these things but these were different kids and this was a heavily female-driven show. Yet, something about the energy of the cast made me feel very suited to them.

First-Time Director

What would you say to the first-time director?

Wow. First-time director is a nasty proposition. First of all, as I already mentioned, I'd make sure that you went in and spent, if you have the time, time with the show. Go down and watch them shoot the previous episode. Once again, get to meet your AD. Get to meet the producers, get to meet the cast. Get to meet them in a place where you kind of schmooze with them while the other poor director is working. He's got to actually do the work [*laughs*]. You're basically already meeting everybody and glad-handling and getting people to support you in your effort that's coming up…. You begin to see how that specific show does it. At that particular point, you have to stay within those parameters.

It's much more specific in single camera but you don't come in as the director to a show like *ER* and determine you no longer want to use handheld. You're now deciding you're not going to shoot it that way. Well, you can't do that! Your job is to find out the system that they employ and to learn their system and do their system as well as you possibly can. If you do that, your chances of succeeding are much better.

Because you're a guest.

Because you're a guest. You have to be thankful that they've allowed you into their house. Try to do things their way. Maybe I'll add a little sprinkle of something that's my own. Like I said, my own style will be imbued in this and sometimes some people's styles work really well and the company says, "Oh, this person is fun." Like I hit with *Laverne & Shirley*, they thought I was out of my mind. They just thought it was so funny that I was so fast.

First-time directors really have to try to get into the way they do it and then add a little personality and style to it. Don't try to make it your own first. That's a big mistake. You can't tell the actors how to play characters they've been playing for three years. You can't say, "Well, I don't want you sitting there this time." That's wrong. Usually if they're sitting at the table in the same place for 300 episodes, you don't want to come in and tell them to sit someplace else at the table. That's just a stupid thing to be doing as a first-time director. That's not where you're going to show that you've got some style and some pizzazz. You can use it other places. But the fact is, you've got to be safe. You've got to shoot the show and you've got to shoot the coverage.

When do you get to show your style and pizzazz?
Usually you get a first chance [as director on a particular series] either because you are an actor on the show and you already know everybody or you are the AD on the show and you already know everybody. Or you're the editor of the show. It's very rare that somebody who has no connection to the show, gets a first show. We had one this year because of a Director's Fellowship program. Kimberly came by and she was charming. She spent weeks watching. She schmoozed. The girls liked her. The cast liked her. She was an actress for many, many years and a successful one.

She became familiar with everybody before Day 1 and made an effort to become part of the family. That's what happens with sitcoms. Families develop.
It's the way the business works, no question. If you're coming into somebody's family, you have to find some time to get in there and schmooze with them. Figure out how they do it. Because that's what your job is. You're not the visionary in a sitcom. You're not coming in with "I have a vision."

On that note, getting closer to your actors can be a form of directing.
My thing is, I like to play along with the actors. I guess I think I'm not much older than some of the kids I direct. I also feel that it's necessary to create a personal relationship because you want to find out who these people are, what their dreams and hopes and aspirations are, what their skills are. I was working on *The Jamie Foxx Show*, totally blown away by the fact that this comedian of comedians was a remarkable singer-pianist. He graduated from a conservatory in Texas, not a college, a conservatory, because his skill level on the piano was that great.

Joel's Approach to the Sitcom

I also find out that he's quite a remarkable football player and all of a sudden he gets cast in *Any Given Sunday* as the quarterback. He's got nobody else there who would go out with him during lunch and play catch. I go, "Okay, come on, Jamie. Let's get out there and play some catch." As he's trying to get his arm loose, he's throwing 60-yard bombs at me and I walk away after lunch with a bruise on my sternum I could not believe. Every time I would catch the ball, I would have to run it back 30 yards so I could get it back to him, then run back 30 yards so he can throw another bomb at me which I would catch in my sternum. I'd pick it up, I'd run it all the way back to him, throw a 20-yard pass and run back. This was my lunch hour.

The bonding was critical. These things pay off in careers. The bonding you do with people, not just Jamie Foxx but the bonding I did with Tom Hanks on *Bosom Buddies* paid off with a little project called *My Big Fat Greek Wedding* that he wanted me to be a part of because of our bonding on *Bosom Buddies*. It goes through your career forever. It's a people-driven place and all things being equal we will go with the people who we like, we will go with the people who like us. We want to create family.

Situation comedy is about family. We had a goodbye party for *Shake It Up* where they just kept it very simply to the cast. Rob Lotterstein, the executive producer of the show, said something during that particular event that I never knew he thought. I never even thought about it myself. He said, "We did not become a family until Joel showed up on that show. That's when we became a family. He was inclusive of everybody. Everybody was part of the family and everybody had their role to play in the family." I was blown away with that. I just do what I do but I think maybe he was right. I wanted to know how those kids were doing in school. I was with their mothers and fathers and talking to them about their personal lives. I was working the parents and working everybody and creating a huge family for it.

That's what situation comedy is and if you really want to have a good time—I'm not saying successful, but if you really want to have a good time doing situation comedy, it's got to be a family environment. You got to be going to work just to have fun. What other job puts you in a place where your whole job is to laugh all day long? That's what situation comedy is about. If you have these other skills that can possibly get you there, boy, that's a wonderful direction to go in.

First-Time Director

A director coming onto a show as a guest needs to be willing to take on the role of stepparent: creating a sense of respect but also knowing how to create boundaries. Being a people person is essential, especially in comedy, because once everybody is comfortable with you and you're comfortable with them, the comedy becomes easier, don't you think?

Much easier. You have to "create" as a director. I always feel my primary responsibility is to create the environment that is necessary for creative funny work to exist, for everybody to be given a chance to do what he or she does best. For me to try to make sure that I help them be the best they can be and I have to do that through setting a feeling on the stage that creates an environment for success for the actors, success for the crews and success for the writer-producers. That becomes critical. You can't do this in a void. You'll have to somehow be in control of that. That's primarily a director's responsibility besides making thousands of decisions in the course of a week. You have to create an environment so everybody does his or her best work.

When I walked in on *Laverne & Shirley* right at the beginning of my career, I had to get a sense of who Penny and Cindy were and who Michael McKean and David Landers [Lenny and Squiggy] were. I just basically went to my instincts from my theater directing in terms of how to deal with them as artists. For the most part they took me to college so it wasn't that easy. They knew exactly how it had to be done. The greatest anecdote from *Laverne & Shirley* is, I have enormous energy.

I remember the girls at that time were having trouble because they were in some fight with the network, in a fight with Paramount. They were unhappy because those were the days when women were not getting their fair share of the revenue compared to the boys. I remember that *Laverne & Shirley* was number one, *Happy Days* was number two, Henry Winkler and Ron Howard were making twice the salary of Penny and Cindy. So Penny and Cindy along with Suzanne Somers on *Three's Company* started to fight the system and said, "No, no, no, not right," so I would sometimes lose them for an entire morning of rehearsal while they were out fighting the system. Then they'd come in and they would just be very pleased to have somebody with a nimble mind, let's call it that, who basically could see what they were doing and adapt to it in five seconds and get it done. So they enjoyed having me because I covered a lot of their needed time to battle the battles, shall we say.

Joel's Approach to the Sitcom

Did they create any obstacles?

No obstacles. They didn't know anything. They had a very good director in Alan Rafkin who'd been with them for the entire second season and he was retiring. Alan had some health issues and it was time for him to go bye-bye, so they had nobody in mind.

They'd been told that I was this young, hot (although not so young and maybe not that hot) director in town who wanted to give a shot on *Laverne & Shirley* and all I was signed up for was two episodes, the first two episodes. And within the first two episodes they had signed me for the rest of the season. Because they liked my energy, they liked the fact that I liked funny and they liked the fact that I laughed at things that I found funny, which I did. I didn't work at that. I just found these guys funny and I would laugh every time Lenny and Squiggy showed up on that set. They would put me away. I'd have a hard time catching my breath with their hello jokes and what have you.

It was my love of comedy that basically endeared me to that particular cast and little by little I got better at camera blocking, I got better at this, I got better at that. I still say to this day Penny and Cindy taught me the ropes, they taught me exactly what it was about staging a sitcom, why this cross should go to the kitchen, why they should be in the living room, etc. They could have staged it all by themselves without a director. So I wasn't sitting there arguing with them, "No, no, no, I don't think you should go to the refrigerator. Why don't you just cross down to the door instead?" I would have never done that and to this day I don't do that.

Basically, if an actor has an impulse, I take a look at the impulse unless it is so far out of the ordinary they can have their impulse. If I feel it's six or one half-dozen, then cross to the refrigerator. I'm not going to be micromanaging that kind of activity and certainly not with successful actors like Penny and Cindy or Ron Howard and Henry Winkler or even Tom Hanks who was a young kid at that time. Hanks was basically 21 years old and had never done anything and I still for the most part wouldn't tell these people what to do. I'd wait to see what it was they did and if I had some funny ideas that I thought that might be entertaining, they would get, "Oh, oh, oh, wait, let's do that. We can do that." But you have to like people, you have to love comedy and ... you have to be a laugher. The actors like it when you laugh at them.

So you have to like yourself and you have be comfortable in your own skin, to be able to come on to a new set and be authentic.

A must.

And once the actors sense your genuine self, that's how relationships start.

Makes a big difference. If you can find a way to tap into who the hell you are and be that person.... I had crazy years in my early years, I was irascible and I would explode and I would do stupid things and I basically had a period of time where I was *persona non grata* at Paramount.

I had been doing *Laverne & Shirley*, I did the pilot of *Bosom Buddies*, I was doing very successful work for Paramount when all of a sudden I got an offer from Witt-Thomas to go over and do *It's a Living* and they were going to make me a producer as well as the director. So I went to that show and when Gary Nardino heard that, he informed everybody, "Zwick is not to be allowed back on the lot again." Luckily, I had Bob Boyette and Tom Miller who was going into the second season of *Bosom Buddies* say, "Listen, we gotta have Zwick back. This is crazy. What are you driving us nuts for?" And they overrode Nardino's objections and I got back into the Paramount family.

You have to survive your youth. You have to survive your youth as a youth. You have to survive your youth as a director, as a professional, because we all make mistakes along the way. We become adamant about things. We become passionate about things we have no business being passionate about and as we get older and we mellow and realize where the humanity of the situation has to occur, we mellow. I've always said that the key is to survive your youth.

Tell me about Tom Hanks and Happy Days.

Basically, one of the things we begin to understand in this business is that personal connections mean everything, they really do, and that people who like you want you to work with them. Well, I was the one who basically called up Tom to inform him that he had *Bosom Buddies*, so we became friendly through that particular period of time. Now, Tom by this point had been finished with *Bosom Buddies*, and essentially he was not doing sitcom any more. One day I'm having breakfast with Bobby Hoffman, who cast both *Laverne & Shirley* and *Happy Days*. He was the main casting director for Gary

Marshall, and Bobby was saying to me that he was very disappointed that they just offered a guest starring role to Tom to play a foil for Henry Winkler in an episode of *Happy Days*, and he turned it down. I said, "Wow. That just doesn't sound like Tom, especially if Henry went out of his way to say, 'I really want Tom to do this role.'" I said, "Before you do anything, let me give Tom a call, and see what this is all about."

I called up Tom, and I said, "Tom, are you aware that you turned down an episode of *Happy Days*?" And Tom said, "I never heard that I was offered an episode of *Happy Days*." Well, Tom fired his agents. I know who they are, but I won't mention them now. He fired his agents. He did *Happy Days*. He met Ron Howard. He met the writers of the movie *Splash*, Lowell Ganz and Babaloo Mandel, and got *Splash*.

***Because of* Happy Days?**
Because of that *Happy Days* episode that he went and did plus his innate talent. But the fact remains that if he hadn't got into that situation where he got to really play with all those guys, *Splash* wasn't going to happen.

A lot of actors, and a lot of A-list feature film actors, did situation comedies. Brad Pitt did **Head of the Class.**
That's right. A little guy by the name of Robin Williams developed a very nice feature career, and somebody by the name of George Clooney, who was a regular on *The Facts of Life*, thank you very much.

But the point of being a director, and the fact that you were sitting with the casting director, not every director coming into situation comedy has those opportunities. Is there a way to create them?
I'd meet Bobby Hoffman every once in a while, because he'd be casting a *Laverne & Shirley*, and then I thought, "Hey, I like Bobby Hoffman," so we'd go have breakfast together, because we were two guys who always got in early. It's that kind of thing.

How did you develop those pivotal relationships?
I just like to meet people. I like people. I want to know who they are. I want to know what they do. I'm interested in, "How's the house going for your

mom"? "Is she coming over from Hawaii?" I want to know these stories about people, because I care about people. I care about the entire crew. I know them all by name, and that crew follows me into Hell, because they're friends of mine. I don't go out to dinner with them, there's no time for dinners, but the fact is, I want to know who everybody is. I want to know little things about them, and if I'm there from six o'clock to nine o'clock in the morning, and all I'm dealing with are construction people and painters, I know everything about their lives. I know who they are. I know who they're married to. I know what marriage it is, and how many kids they've got, what problems they're going through right now, because I just make it my business to do that, because I happen to like knowing about people. I do the same thing with actors. Just recently I was doing an episode of *Jessie*, and [actress] Leigh-Allyn Baker was given a chance to direct an episode of *Jessie*. She was coming around to basically observe me, and also to meet the cast, to meet the crew, to do all that. Despite the fact that she was already given this opportunity, she didn't have to fight for it, because she had done a couple of episodes of [the TV series] *Good Luck Charlie* and so she came in and paid some dues—I mean, schmoozing everybody.

Now, schmoozing may be thought of by some to be a questionable word, but no. She was talking up to people, and meeting the camera operators, and the camera coordinator ... she's one of those people who does that. She is one of these people who goes out, and meets, and greets, and is happy to do that, and that's going to pay off. I think that crew on *Jessie* will have her back when she shows up. Whatever lack of skill she may have with camera, or lack of skill she may have with this or that, they're going to have her back.

Trust the Crew

What other advice do you have for the first-time director of a show when it comes to the crew?

Well, no director does it all. The best directors are the ones who know how to assign responsibility to responsible people and let them do their job. The example I use is: I know that Steven Spielberg does not bring John Williams in to write the score for *Schindler's List* and then sit there and hum it to him. He's got an artist on his hands and that artist will go off and come up with something based on talks he's had with Steven Spielberg about how to score *Schindler's List*. The same thing goes on any level. You have to have total respect for the people who are working around you. You must. You have to instill it, you have to instill in them the belief that you think they're good enough to do the best job possible. The *Shake It Up* crew is unbelievable, how good they are. If I had them on my features, I would have done those features in one-third the time! These guys are that good and that efficient. Because we give them their head. We let them do their job and we ask for their input and we encourage them and we're lucky to have them.

I don't have to make all those decisions. I have to simply be sure that I'm on top of all decisions that are being made by the best people that can possibly make them, which is not me. You as the assistant director got a list ... there is stuff about actors, schedules and school and stuff like that. I couldn't do that job in a million years, that attention to detail. It would knock me out. But I don't think about it for a second. I know that I'm going to get from you the maximum amount of time you can wring out for me to be able to do the work that I need to do. I'm not going to question you on it. I don't come to you and say, "Hey, wait a second, why can't I get 15 more minutes with that kid?" I know by now that you have figured out that that was the optimum deal that I could get. I just take it and run with it and do not put my energy into worrying about those things. You've just have too many other things to worry about. You can't do other people's jobs for them.

You've come to the point in your career where you know that you can trust departments to do what they do. You can trust the first AD to run the stage, but again, there's that sense of trust that also has to be earned.

Darn right so.

It behooves the first-timer to know that when you do come onto a show, you are a guest. Trust the routine of the show and don't take anything personally. There was one instance where a guest director wanted to do something that was outside of the show's established parameters. I advised him accordingly, but he took it personally. I was actually helping him, but unfortunately, he didn't seem to understand that. I'm not even sure this

director is aware of the rationale but I continued to do my job and forge forward with the same guidance offered to all directors.

You cannot change the way the show is being operated because you're going to get guff from actors, you're going to get guff from the producers, you're going to get guff from the crew, nobody's going to be really happy with you if you try to change things. The system has been in place for years and they're not looking for some person to show up and reinvent the system. This also ties into the amount of power you have and, let's face facts, as a first-time hire to direct a sitcom, you have no power. You're a very lucky person to get a shot and you have to understand what you have to do politically. What you have to do socially. You just bring whatever craft you've got to bear and get the job done. Trust the professionals around you who have been doing the show to do the show. All you have to do is get in there and direct and it'll make your life a lot easier than trying to change the system or doing other people's jobs for them.

Step 1: Preparation

Day 1: Meetings and Rehearsal

Arriving early to stage on Monday to walk the show's sets before the production meeting, table read and rehearsal is an important factor in the process of directing a situation comedy. You want to get familiar with the sets and make notes in your script for the production meeting and table read based on your initial breakdown of your ideas and how you interpret the script. In this chapter we look at how preparation creates the basis for success, and ultimately leads to career longevity in the world of sitcoms.

Production Meeting: Prep and Execution

Previous to the production meeting, usually what happens is at least two days beforehand I get a script, a writer's draft arrives usually by email. At that point I have to get into the script and take a look at the script because I know my first responsibility is going to be to get down to the sets, check out the sets and run a production meeting.

Most of my homework for that production meeting is done as soon as I get that first written script. I look through it, I make decisions as to whether there are big production problems and then I basically take a yellow marker and I mark everything in the script that's production-oriented, be it a prop that's being specifically asked for, or the time of day. Is it a day scene or a night scene? Anything that will affect wardrobe? Does it involve a special effects man who has to be on the set, or a choreographer as we did every week on *Shake It Up*? How does that all manipulate in. You've been very helpful because you'll have much more specific concerns like, how many extras am I getting? What is the breakdown of the additional dancers? That's my AD's job to have my back. My organizational concerns are bigger than that. I sit at home and I study the script and practically memorize it and that job used to take me forever. It's no longer taking me forever but the fact is, I still get in early. If the production meeting is nine o'clock in the morning, you can bet your bottom dollar I'm on set at about seven o'clock. I'm walking the sets. The crew is there still building the sets for the episode for crying out loud and I'm walking the sets. I'm talking to the construction crew: "Why is that wall there? Why do we have a wall there? I don't need a wall there." [*Laughs*]

My guy Scotty Hansen says, "Okay, let's get rid of the wall. He doesn't want the wall." I'd short-circuit physical problems that I see in the sets that they're building because I already have an idea in my head from studying the script how I think the scenes are going to have to play out.

I start to get input into the sets and into how they are dressed because in situation comedy you don't shoot actors, you shoot sets. Especially when you have four cameras to manipulate, you have to have set pieces in places where those cameras can shoot; otherwise it takes you forever to shoot a scene. That's not the point of a situation comedy. It must be moving rapidly enough to keep the humor and the excitement alive. If it dredges on too long, it saps the energy of the actors and you never get the kind of buoyant performances that comedy usually needs. Speed is not a panacea but with financial budgets and time restrictions on talent, you have to be efficient in trying to get the job done.

Mechanics of the Production Meeting and Making Decisions

You mentioned you work from the writer's draft. What about the set plans? Are they mailed to you?
No.

You don't deal with the plans? Do you look at the plans?
No. By the time I get the plans, I've already seen the sets. Unless there's something they come to me specifically for, that they had to clear plans with me because of some problems, something that they anticipated, I don't see plans. I am not involved at all in the design of these sets. That's a job done

Step 1: Preparation

primarily by the co-executive producers like Frank Pace. Essentially these sets are designed and for the most part planned for in terms of how they're going to be dressed long before I'm involved in the situation.

But I'd asked you questions before you got involved and you already knew the length of a wall that was needed. You knew the wall that was needed was eight feet, not 12 feet. You did your work not off of a plan but in your head when you were on the set.
Yes, exactly.

Once again, it was your third eye. So you visualized the set off of a one-dimensional piece of paper and you waited until it was three-dimensional.
Yes. That's why I show up two hours before the production meeting, to make sure that if I have a real visualization of a scene and if the set doesn't seem to be fulfilling the needs, I get into that pretty quickly as to exactly what the producers wanted because obviously I'm not seeing what they wanted or if I am seeing what they wanted, they better change the set because I can't shoot that thing that they're trying for in that space. That comes with a little experience but essentially that's what I do.

Then I get into the production meeting. It's an hour long and you better get through the production meeting, this is not time for playing games. I tend to run the production meetings although in many sitcoms the first AD will run the production meeting or a producer might run a production meeting. I like to do it because, once again, it helps me learn the script.

As I go through the script and say, "Okay, it's Day 1. Day 1, we're in the living room and they're going to be eating a healthy salad and studying with their books and computers." Now I got that visually and I start to plant that in my head and I go through every page. Page by page with every little yellow highlighted mark in the script that I've got that might suggest, "Oh, we're going to need a banana for this scene, guys. She peels a banana in this scene."

Everybody else in the production meeting has done their homework and props already been through the script and they know what they're supposed to do. Wardrobe has already been through the script and they know what they need to do. Sets are being built and designed and dressed so they know what they're doing. This is basically a forum so that everybody gets on the same page.

Mechanics of the Production Meeting and Making Decisions

What else happens during the production meeting?

Any outstanding questions will get answered. We have specific production problems that were unique to our show. We have the problem of the dance each week and "How many hours of rehearsal are we going to have to allot to that?" and "How many dancers are they going to be giving and are those dancers boys or girls?" That has to be all worked out at the production meeting. Obviously by this point we already know how much time we're going to allot for the dances because that's what we allot for dance rehearsal.

[Choreographers are] going to get our actors but you're also dealing with three hours of school and you're dealing with only nine and a half hours for 15-year-olds and only ten and a half hours for 16-year-olds in the course of a given day due to child labor laws, and you're playing all kinds of production games that are the bailiwick of the first AD and maybe a producer, but certainly I'd stay out of that. I'd drive myself nuts if I try to retain information about all that stuff that you have in your brain. Not a shot in Hell. I have to focus very specifically on my job and I have to delineate that and let everybody else do their job and then hopefully if they gave me good enough people, the job will be done well.

What I always believed about directing is that the director's main responsibility is to make decisions, make them quickly, make them efficiently, and in that way he sets the tone for how he runs his set. It does not matter if they're right or wrong. If they're wrong, somebody else will say, "Joel, by the way that's a stupid decision. Why don't we go with this instead?" You certainly have a track record of doing that with me.

The fact is, I will start that decision-making process. I will say, "We're going to go to yubaba." At which point now all of a sudden people start to get interested. But yubaba. Do we really want to go to yubaba? Can't we just as easily go to bubba? And the game gets played. That's a living, breathing organism in a relationship that's played out based on everybody who now interacts within the system, understanding the system and the parameters of the system and what their specific job is in the system with me at the helm.

So you're making those initial decisions in the production meeting, so the department heads have the specifics.

For example, if the prop master has to make a robot, he now knows how

Step 1: Preparation

big, what color and what it's supposed to do mechanically, based on what you're expecting.

Or in this case, it can also be what the writers are expecting. They will have expected as they've written in the script a robot who knocks at the door and hands him pizza. Okay, I'm working with props and I'd go, "Well, we're never going to get that kind of robot. Well, what can we get out of this robot?" Therefore, I would help build the moment on stage with what is more realistically capable of being done and the writer will go, "Okay, fine, that's good." Always remember the writers also have a vision of things they want to see accomplished in a scene and my job is not only to tell their story but to also help fulfill their vision. I have to try to get their vision, which they have clearly marked out in the script, by giving stage directions. In the production meeting they talk about props that they're interested in. They're talking about "Don't let her wear yellow outfits. She looks horrible in yellow. Let's make sure she's in pink this week," or whatever that's all about. All that input comes and has to be handled by all the department heads and we move on from there.

Also with wardrobe, you know in your head what's needed because you pre-block the scenes before the meeting. You ask, "Is this actress wearing a skirt?, because I'm intending to have her come through a window, then I'm intending to have her sit on the couch where she's facing camera." How many times did Jessica Replansky, our costume designer, say, "Well, yes, the outfit that we have, she does wear a skirt." Since that's not always practical, it's something that needs to be addressed.

Yes, with Leggings. Perhaps you're going to have to do something because she needs to be physical in this scene. It's dealing with the physical nature of the show, but the costume department by now is pretty hip. Jessica will now always come to me and say, "Is there any reason I can't put her in a skirt for this scene?" I'd go, "No, you can put her in a skirt." We'll get that negotiated but those are the things that get done at the production meeting, and "Should there be any more involvement in special effects?" [You meet] with special effects people to discuss exactly how something is done. That takes up time. So, usually we'll do sidebars because it takes up too much of everybody's time during the meeting as to exactly how we're going to go about dealing with this special effect if it's either a physical special effect or if it's a visual one where they're going to have to do some [post-production] work for us, they're going to have to tell me how I shoot that so they get the information they need in order to do the visual work, the CGI [computer-generated imagery] or or whatever it is that they're going to do. They will be part of the process of how that's shot so that that can be accomplished. That's another responsibility of mine: to listen to all that input and make sure that I am servicing the need. If I don't give them the footage they need to do the work they're supposed to do, I wouldn't be working very often in the business.

Right. If the executive producers wrote a special effect into the script we would normally have the special effects people at the meeting, especially if it's a complex effect that might require special attention.
You betcha.

Then the dialogue begins on how to create this effect.
It's very hard to translate a concept in a weekly sitcom. Easier maybe if you're shooting for a year on a movie, but very hard to translate the specifics of a visual effect. Some are easier to understand, the ones that are done all the time. Sometimes it's more complicated and getting on the same page does take time and energy. Once the special effects are on the clock, they're actually busy every day to make sure that things are being set up properly, or execution of a stunt and making sure it's safe and getting the stunt coordinator down on stage and getting the stunt people to do their work. That's their responsibility.

I'm not staging stunts. I am talking to the stunt coordinator about, "It'll be great if we could...," "Is it possible to do this?" Just like I would talk to a choreographer and tell him, "Listen. I got to contain this dance. You're spreading too much on me. I'll get a much better movie of this dance if I can tighten it up and not let you spread it all over the place which isn't helping me."

In the production meeting, the choreographer also describes the concept, so that you have a mutual understanding of how the dancing will be incorporated into the show. This also applies to any fight choreography and stunts.
All visuals are conceptual right at the beginning and then they morph on us. Any visual concept begins to grow as we spend some time on it within

Step 1: Preparation

the next few days and really develop the finesse of what that's going to be and how we're going to shoot that and how we're going to rehearse that and how many people are there and "Wait a second, you mean that man in the yellow raincoat has to stand there for this to happen? How the hell am I supposed to shoot around him?" Those things have to be worked out. Obviously, the more experience you have, the more you see all the potential places where you got to put energy into the production meeting to make sure that that production is going to happen.

Special Equipment

There may be special equipment for any given episode, especially when you're shooting a dance show like *Shake It Up*, the possibility of bringing in a jib that's a high angle arm that can sweep around and do fancy shots from way above. Perhaps we're going hand-held in certain sequences. Perhaps we haven't done it on *Shake It Up* but I've done in other shows, bringing in a Steadicam for certain kinds of things, or a slow-motion camera. That's the equipment that's available to us on sitcoms that people are using nowadays pretty regularly.

Most sitcoms are sitting around with a jib waiting to be used. But still it's a four-camera situation so that you still have four camera operators with them. At any given time you can only shoot four shots at the same time, but the fact remains that you do have the possibility of swinging a camera to a jib instead of using the traditional pedestal (ped).

You might take a camera off of a Ped and let it go hand-held. You might do any number of things but that's equipment. That's the concerns in the production meeting. Will there be any specialized needs in terms of equipment that we must rent or bring in for this particular week's episode?

These are things that you would bring into the production meeting.
Yes. I'd bring my needs into the production meeting but for the most part, the people who are involved are smart enough to know this show that this particular episode will need a jib. They're smart enough to know that and every once in a while there will be a negotiation because of financial or because of this or of that, because of budgetary needs as to how much equipment we

bring in and the cost of this equipment and how often can we use this equipment. That has to be negotiated, that is a political thing that has to be dealt with. You can't walk off and say, "I'm the director and if I don't get a jib I'm not coming back tomorrow." Chances are you won't come back tomorrow and you won't come back the next day and you will never come back again. Basically, you have your wants and your desires but it's within a political framework of people who are making decisions based on budget needs, based on this, based on that, and you take that into your account. You still have your needs and you should express them as a director but don't be surprised if they don't care about your needs. They just care about their needs.

Visualization of the Set

Talk about how the sets are visualized in the production meeting.

The biggest problem tends to be the visualization of swing sets. A swing set is a set that's not your normal standing set. It's not your living room and kitchen or the school place or Crusty's Pizza on *Shake It Up*. It's a brand new space. Usually the concept of what that looks like comes from the executive producing writer, that head writer in our case for *Shake It Up* was Rob Lotterstein. He would visualize this set as being whatever he visualizes and he will communicate his visualization of this set to Greg Richman, the set designer, to Daryn Goodall our set decorator and Natalie Contreras and the rest of the art department team. He will communicate directly to them what he thinks he wants.

I say "thinks he wants" because that's where sometimes the communication breaks down where the people who are producing the swing set are not quite giving the executive producer what he thought he was getting. We did one recently where it was a Sweet 16 party set and they came up with furniture that the executive producer hated. Hated the look. Just wouldn't deal with it. Daryn had to go back to square one and find something closer. Rob was finally able to communicate to him what it is that he was looking for so Daryn went out and got it.

My job is not so much whether it's Louis XIV period furniture or supermodern or anything like that, couldn't care less about that. It's not my world. They make decisions about that. What I care about is the ground plan. I want to know where the couch is that I can cross people to. I want to know if there are chairs over there that I can do this with. I want to know if I've got tables in the foreground. I want to know if I can make this world work. I'm not interested in what color they paint their walls. Somebody else would be interested and they should be but that doesn't interest me.

My interest is in the movement of a scene, the kinetics of a scene, and I have to have my furniture in places where I can send people where I know I can shoot them and I can make this kinetic movie because, let's face facts, grand vision in sitcoms doesn't exist. There's no grand vision. It's "Get the coverage," one or two really nice shots that surprise people and get on with it. You're not going to get a grand vision. You're not shooting on top of the Eiffel Tower to all of Paris. You don't get those kind of things. You're shooting essentially in sitcom, a three-walled set.

So, it's set up like the proscenium in theater where the cameras and the audience are all viewing from one open space and the rest of the world is happening in a 260-degree or 270-degree frame. You can come around a little bit but the fact is, 180 degrees is really what you're doing and that's what the nature is. The way sitcom has evolved is, every once in a while sets will come up which actually need a fourth wall but you gotta find a way to open it up a little bit. Like when you shot a table scene in the episode you directed, you had to bring in a fourth wall, otherwise there was no way to shoot those people around the table. That comes up but that's infrequent, especially for a show that is a laugh track sitcom.

The Table Read

When I prepare for the production meeting, I'm preparing at the same time for the table read because I have to underline and yellow-highlight all the things that I will read in terms of stage direction. Because at a table read, nobody's acting out the scene so therefore the action of the scenes that needs to be read has to be read by the director in my case. Sometimes other people have people read. I read stage direction because I like to energize the read.

My energy, which is my best asset, is very useful at a table read because I can drive a scene or drive something through by reading the stage direction

The Table Read

with enough passion or enough emotion or enough something to show the actors the kind of attack they must have on a scene. So I have that all marked out and I know exactly which ones I read. Then I basically improvise with the actors. If they're on a roll and I don't get to say a stage direction, so I didn't say it or whatever. I'll feel that out as we go but I'm planning to just be there with them at the reading and I'll be their voice. I'll read their stage directions and inspire them to do whatever it is that I can inspire them to do at a reading so that the writers get the best reading they possibly can get so they see what they've got on their hands.

So, in a production meeting you're looking for answers to technical questions. Now you are the commander of this table read and how you're dealing with the talent, which is a different animal altogether from the production meeting.

The talent has gotten scripts beforehand. They have looked over the scripts. If they were confused, they have their dialogue coach who will answer questions for them. If there's pronunciation of words that concern them or if there's beats or moments in the script that they don't understand, they will come to me before the reading or go to somebody else and ask to have it explained. So they've done a little homework. This is not a cold reading. This is a reading of people who have read the script and who have committed, to some degree, to some choices that they're already interested in.

Do you talk about those choices before the table read?

No I don't. I'm interested in what they want to do. However, if they come to me and they say, "Excuse me but I really have no idea what the writer is talking about here," I will try to get them through that so they can get it for the table read. And usually the writers are smart enough to hear it at the table read and go, "Whoops, we're going to rewrite that." Like with everything else, I'm not there to tell the actors what to do. I'm there to let the actors be the best they can be and in my estimation if you let actors have their head, so to speak, allow them to make their own choices to fail if they must and to succeed brilliantly when they do, then you're building an actor who basically is in control of his or her own destiny. They know what they want to do and therefore from that point on, all you're doing is molding a little bit of clay. You're not

Step 1: Preparation

telling people what to do. Hopefully they've already decided. What they decided to do is the best choice and you're just pulling those best choices together and making it come together. That takes a little bit of confidence as a director to realize that you've got to leave it in the hands of the actors, especially if they've played a character for three years.

Sometimes you don't, though. *Shake It Up* is a unique situation in that you start off with girls who were 13 and by the time you're finished they're 16. If you think they're anything like they were at 13, you haven't raised a daughter because that feels like 17 years in their lives. It's unbelievable, the changes that go on. At that point as they're morphing into older kids, they're moving from tweeners to teenagers, from teenagers to young ladies, you're there with the writers or helping coach the writers along to get these characters more mature so they're not 19 years old playing 11. Basically you need to do a little bit more work with the actors at that stage as they're developing their aging characters.

I remember going to Zendaya, who played Rocky on *Shake it up*, at one point and saying, "Excuse me, but as far as I can tell you're half black. I see your father. I see your mother. I want to know, where is the black in this character? I have never seen any black in this character. You're playing a little white girl and I don't know why you're doing that. I see attitudes all over the stage that I never seen in your performance. Some of those have got to start to come into your performance." Sure enough, it started to develop. All of a sudden her takes, her attitudes were much sharper. She found a way to infuse a little bit of soul into a character that she didn't know she should be doing.

So, yeah, every once in a while you do speak to an actor about something like that, but for the most part I let them wallow in their own choices. Wallow. Let them make mistakes. Let them succeed and then we'll help them out after they've wallowed.

The Pilot: How You Can Help Shape a Show

Let's say someone is a seasoned director, who's proven themself and gained the trust of the networks and executive producers, has an opportunity to do a pilot. The production meetings are the same. But what should they do differently for the pilot before the table read?

The Pilot: How You Can Help Shape a Show

Usually in a pilot, the director is brought into casting which is not something that happens in episodic because if you're directing every episode of a series, you have no time to go to casting and the cast is already there. You come into a show with a cast in place and any guest cast is hired by the executive producer.

For pilots, you are in all the casting sessions. Some of it's based on names that are being drawn in that are signed on to do the pilot that the pilot is being done because of them or with them and some of them are through an audition process. So you've been watching these actors go through network auditions and studio auditions and all kinds of auditions so you have a pretty good idea of what the talent pool is and what these actors are going to bring. Maybe you've done some screen tests on them to see what they look like on camera. Therefore you know them a little bit better.

Then my job as a director of a pilot is different in that my job there is to take five actors who have never been working together before and somehow mold them into an ensemble in the amount of time I've got to create an energy that gets all those actors willing to play with each other and to challenge each other and to be there for each other. If you can find a way in your style to make that happen. To generate that from a bunch of actors who just met two weeks before, well, then you've got yourself something on your hands. That sense of ensemble is essentially what sells most of these pilots. Because the company looks like they've been together for a year.

But you're not doing that alone. You're doing that with the executive producer and creator.

Oh yes. You're doing it with creators who are writing and continuing to write and to shape. Good example: We were doing *Perfect Strangers*. We're reshooting the pilot which had been done one way and now we've brought Mark Linn-Baker to play opposite Bronson Pinchot for the reshoot. We're doing a scene and the scene is over and I'm in a break. I look over there and there is Bronson and Mark doing all kinds of stupid stuff. They're slapping each other, they're grabbing ties. They had this whole physical vocabulary that just came naturally to them. I looked over there and I said, "Oh, gee whiz." I called up the exec producers, Bill Bickley and Michael Warren, and I said, "You guys have got to get down to the set. I've got to show you what these guys do when nobody's paying any attention to them." They came down to the set and they looked over and said, "Oh my God." And they turned it from a verbal comedy into a physical comedy with dancing and singing and all kinds of silliness. That emerged simply because I saw these two clowns off in a corner playing games with each other while they were on a five-minute break.

So that is an avenue where you can flex your muscles as a director and to actually infuse some of your creative voice.
Very much so.

Which is normally not the case. The pilot is unique. It's an opportunity; it's very much like a feature film because you have a voice in shaping ...
You will never see that much voice again unless they then hire you to be the director for the series. That's a two-way street. There was a time in the Miller-Boyett years where directors were hired to do an entire series. I did four years of *Perfect Strangers*. I did four years of *Full House* and I mean full years. I was the director for those shows. That was the way Bickley-Warren liked to work. That was the way that Miller-Boyett liked to work. They wanted a strong director on the floor to work with the actors and to build that show from the floor up.

Then you work with other producers who basically want more voice so they don't want the same director every week. If they can hire a director for two episodes here, one episode there, the director becomes beholden and will not be that strong a voice on the floor. The voice will be that of the executive producers.

Obviously the bigger the track record you have and the more people know you and know the quality of your work, you can get away with things that a novice better not even try and that another director wouldn't dare try. I mean, people kind of know what to expect. Who I am and what I do. I'm not a big secret. If you don't want to be messing around, then hire me. However, it's happened a few times where I've run into a producer in a big meeting and we looked at each other and I could hear him saying, "You know we are not going to work together. It will never happen. I'm much too headstrong, you're much too headstrong. I'm too this, you're too that." We parted company very amicably. So you don't get every job but as long as you've got enough jobs to keep you working, you're doing pretty good.

So creative chemistry is important.

It's a huge thing in how you meld a group of people and how you create a world and an environment for these new actors who haven't worked together before. An environment where they can be creative. Where they can take chances. Where they can fail. Where they can question and get it done in a time frame that has to be done. The parameters of the time don't expand for these things. You have to get it done in the proper amount of time, but you have to get everybody to enjoy taking chances. To enjoy playing with each other. To enjoy failing. Making failing a fun time for everybody. So that they don't feel like their world has ended because they missed a joke. You make fun and you have fun with the fact that they missed a joke. Or the fact is that nobody could have made that joke. That was a stupid joke. Whatever the way you do it to defuse the situation, you get people to take chances. If you can get people to take chances with each other, good actors will amaze you with what they're capable of doing. It blows my mind, good acting!

The Table Read for Your First Time Directing a Show

A director coming on to a show for the first time: After the production meeting what would your advice be to prepare for the table read? What questions should be asked of the executive producers involving the table read and the actors?

Usually at the table read, it is not the appropriate time to be telling producers what you think might be right or wrong with their script. That's just not a good political thing to do. If you have real concerns about understanding a scene or something, go to the executive producer or the writer, one on one, privately, and talk to them because you don't want to do that in a public arena at all. As far as the actors go, I listen to what the actors are doing. Hear the script. Then we send the actors away and do network and producer notes.

Stay out of this. For the most part, save your notes and speak directly to the executive producer afterwards.

Then what I am going to do for the rest of the day is, I'm going to take a look at the scenes that I think will not get rewritten heavily and I will start the rehearsal with the actors, putting them on their feet in these scenes. Yes we understand now that I don't rehearse on the first day because I just think it's a waste of my time; however, in reality, any other director that doesn't do it is a fool. I'm a stager. I'm not there to watch the actors improvise where they want to go. No, no, no, no, I want them to cross to the couch; I'd like them to sit in that chair. I think you can go to the window there, you're crossing to the refrigerator and sit down and have a Coke. There is no game-playing with that. Now, once I got them on their feet and they've seen how I feel that that character should move, once they have that information, and they have tried it, then they can come to me and say, "I tried that but I think it might be better if I just sat down." I go, "You know, you're right.|" The actors can give input after I think they have enough knowledge of what the scene is structurally about, what the scene is trying to do. Now they can play and if that means slight alterations then, we will adapt.

Putting It on Its Feet

Define "putting the play on its feet."

You put the play on its feet so that the writers can see what it is they wrote and therefore they can fix it if they need to. They can tighten it if they need to. They can do better jokes if they need to. They can restructure it if they need to but you've got to get it on its feet so they see their show and not so they are impressed with you as a director. That can't be the name of the game. I think you will lose that game.

Rehearsal Advice for the First-Timer on a Show

What is your advice to the director coming on to an established show about guiding the actors after the table read? You've seen what the actors did or

didn't bring to the table. What worked as a joke and what didn't and why. Now, what advice would you give to these directors about rehearsing?

I believe the director is the audience for the first part and has to respond to the action that is going on. Especially if you're doing a show that has a laugh track, I think it's the responsibility of the director to laugh when he thinks something is funny, to inspire the actors to do something even funnier. So I will watch them doing things and my approach usually isn't to tell them what to do, it's more to ask them what is it that you think you're doing. "What are you playing there? What are you doing? I don't understand what you're doing." "Why wouldn't you just do this? Why are you doing that?" They sometimes will have a very good explanation and you'll go, "Oh! So that's what you think." At that point, I have to look at it with them and see the problem they're having. Okay, we'll tell the producers about this, but right now let's just get through this moment. I'm not going to solve a questionable writing thing. That's going to be up to the writers to solve it. If it's real small, if I've got to bend on something that makes a joke funnier, I'll give it to them.

If there is some line that is so ridiculously out of whack that we can't even get through the scene, I'll remove the line. All this goes into the script and the producers will then take a look at the stage notes that have been modified from the read and they will either include it because they like it in the next draft, which I will get that night, or they will ignore it, which means they didn't like my solution to the problem. But don't do too much of that either. You have to be really very, very specific and very, very sparse with messing around with somebody else's script.

Rehearsing Joel's Style and Actor Resistance

What about when you first came onto Shake It Up? You felt you knew the actors the first time hearing them at the table read.

Yes, I knew exactly who they were and what they brought as actors to the table read.

Now the prep is behind you and it's rehearsal time. How did you handle the actors?

Step 1: Preparation

I say, "It's time to do a scene, we're going to do this scene, okay? I need you sitting on the couch, but I need you in the middle of the couch so that when he comes out he can be sitting next to you there. I'll have you on the counter; you're going to be over there. Okay, give her some tea as it says in the script. You're coming from your room; I'm not reinventing that, come from your room. Your sister's on the couch. You want to talk to your sister, come to the couch and talk to your sister."

It doesn't take a lot of logistics to figure out 90 percent of what the situation comedy staging should be about. The writing is telling you what you're doing. They tell you when they're entering, when they're exiting, where they're entering from and where they're exiting to. These are all givens. There are certain areas where you have a little more creative control as a director, but essentially, my job is, once again, just stage it for the writers.

I'm not trying to invent business at this point. I want to see what they invent themselves and I just let the process go on. On Monday, I'm not looking for a product that I really want when I'm shooting on Thursday or Friday. I just want to get it to the next level where I can show on Tuesday at the run-through for the producers, that their show works, and that these are the areas that are brilliant in it, and there's a few areas which are not working, and they're going to have to address them.

What do you do about any resistance?

From actors? Wow, you don't want to be in a situation where you're hoping that the way you present this stuff won't cause actors to get their hackles up, and to resist. You're hoping that somehow you're going to find a way to kind of negotiate through it. We had an actress I had some problems with at the beginning because she was very strong-minded and very strong-willed and I wanted a process of getting it on its feet first, then entertaining her needs. She wanted to entertain her needs before I got it on its feet. So we were having some problems with process. A few episodes later, we worked that out.

I know she is a person who lives in the real world and wants props. She wants real-world props to play her scenes, and she's a terrific matcher. There is no question that if she picks up a spoon, she's picking up the spoon the exact same time, the exact same way every time so you don't have to worry about handing her props and saying, "Oh my God this is going to be a nightmare." But the fact is, I learned that she needs certain things to feel comfortable when she works and she learned that I need to set the scene. I got kids on the set. I'm not sitting and negotiating with a truly adult, crafty, experienced actress, when I've got kids on the set. That's not the time for that. So eventually, pretty quickly, we worked through that little problem. Yes, that will happen on occasion that my style may rub somebody the wrong way. Not everybody will be signed on to have to work with me, but she began to understand that my job is to work with kids.

What advice would you have for the first-time director coming onto the show regarding this challenge?

If I was a more mellow man, if I wasn't such a complete moron at times, there were better ways to handle some actors than the way I did for sure. I spent a lot of my career apologizing for questionable behavior. But the fact remains that I should have gone into her dressing room and asked if we could talk for a few minutes. Should've said, "We've got to iron this out. I've got these kids on the set. I've got to be able to tell them what exactly to do. It's hard for me to tell them when you won't listen to anything I'm asking you to do. So, we've got to come up with a plan."

It took longer than it should have, but that's what you really need to do as a director. If you're having trouble with some actor in the company, you've got to go meet with him and talk to him, go out to lunch with him. You've got to make it work. Like you say, you as the director are the adult. I don't care how old the actress is, she's the child, or the actor is. You're the adult. It's up to you to make things good.

Like the time you had Alex Karras and Susan Clark who were real-life husband and wife. And they also portrayed a husband and wife on Webster.

They had met during the filming of the movie *Babe,* based on the character Babe Zaharias. Susan Clark played Babe and Alex Karras played her agent or manager or something. They got together and they got married and they had a lovely girl and then they did the sitcom *Webster* together which they co-starred in. Now, the downside of having a husband and wife is: What if they

Step 1: Preparation

have a fight at night? What if they get into some kind of a spat with each other and they bring that to the set?

Did that actually happen?

Yeah! [*Laughs*] What happened is, we have this little scene, I didn't know that they had been in a spat that night, and essentially this was a very simple scene. It couldn't have been more than six, seven lines where Alex's character was supposed to come in to Susan's study where she has her office and simply run a little scene, a few lines. I was about to set up the scene when Alex said, "I'm not walking in that woman's study." I asked, "What woman's study?" He said, "I'm not going to go into that study and talk to that woman." I said, "Alex, it's in the script. You're supposed to walk into the study and you have to engage yourself in the scene with your camera wife." He says, "I'm not going to do it," so I said okay. I go over to Susan and I say, "Susan, you're the rational member of your team. Would you go in to Alex's study and can I do the scene there?" She says, "Absolutely not. It very specifically says in the script, he comes into my study." I said okay. You know how I solved it? I put Alex in his study, I put Susan in her study and I had them do the scene on the phone.

How did you sell that to the producers?

There was no selling. I just had to do it. I said, "If you guys want to try to get into this marital thing, go for it, but let me tell you, if you're smart, you'll just buy the scene like this and let's get on with it."

This was on a shoot day, so you had no recourse.

It had to be done or it wasn't going to be done [*laughs*].

So eventually, the scene worked out?

Yeah, we got it and eventually the two of them figured out their little problems together, but that was one of the few times that I saw that husband-and-wife thing materialize itself in a way that I was not expecting.

Step 2: Staging

Day 2: Building a Solid Foundation

Staging the actors based on the table draft and blue revised table draft so they can best use the set during rehearsal is a key component of Joel's process. He will use different parts of a set if multiple scenes take place in the same set. He feels that putting the teleplay on its feet is one of the most important aspects of the process. Now we'll look at how effectively placing an actor in a set is the key to getting a show shot in the five-day work week. It's a fundamental precept that is essential to building the right foundation for everything else that will follow.

Staging: Set Notes for Camera and First-Time Advice

I, basically, nowadays, do my staging in my mind, but there was a time where I would write little notes on the script to allow for staging. Coming up with the system that's your own, that you think is efficient to use on how you can write down on a piece of paper the fact that it's going to be a two-shot against the one. That's how I write it down, two against one, one against two. Cross three. Cross two. That's all I need if I was going to write anything down to remind me.

Now, even with staging, you arrange furniture to make any physical comedy work and some of your blocking work better. You would be so bold to move some set pieces. Tell me a little about that because you're always thinking about camera the whole time. That's the overall theme, that you're always thinking camera.

I'm making a movie. I'm making my show.

Step 2: Staging

Okay, but now with the staging, you're still putting a play up on its feet.

I have to know it's placed in a spot where I can shoot and get the kind of coverage that I want. The only place that that makes a difference for us really is in Crusty's, the pizza parlor, because I have eight tables floating around. To be quite honest, they could be arbitrarily schlepped around all over the place. I will basically make a decision that, okay, I'm going to do one scene at the counter. I'll do another scene at a table. I will place all these tables where my eye tells me their best place is for shootability. Luckily, through years of knowledge, I can pretty well see what that shot was going to be.

You talk about staging and sets. If you look at ten episodes back to back to back and look at the scenes in the same set, the furniture would not match.

Not necessarily. No.

... because you moved the set pieces.

To accommodate the scene.

... and the script and the staging. And for even first-time directors to know that they can go into a set ...

... and modify the ground plan.

Because set pieces aren't nailed down.

Well, you know what I did in the last episode. I "flattened" the couch—I moved it all around, because I knew I was going to have trouble going in that direction because of the angle of the couch. I was going to have trouble because I don't like the wall behind that shot. I knew that Zendaya was going to be there in a money scene, crying. I knew that she had to be in that spot, so therefore I just took the couch and flattened it so that Gary Allen, my "X" camera operator, now had a great shot of her eyes and she had a background that looked like we're still in the set.

But the importance of that statement is that that couch was always on an angle for the duration of the show. You needed it in this one scene ...

Flattened out.

Staging: Set Notes for Camera and First-Time Advice

Flattened out. Who's going to know?

Nobody's going to know. The old game is that we'll take that letter. It's even worse when you're dealing with the Disney Channel [*laughs*]. Let's just say we'll take that letter from the eight-year-olds, but it's not fair. You still want to do A work. You're always doing A work. Let me say this to any director: You never, ever, ever do anything but your best work. I don't care whether you're doing a show in a slop house in Soho or you're doing the highest-rated television show in history. The same work ethic must be used. You can't dump work. Once you do that, you basically corrupt your soul. You corrupt your artistic soul. If you're willing to blow something because you're bored, because you think it's beneath you, or because you think it's not as elevated a story as you should be doing, that's the end. That's an end position. You can't survive that as an artist. You have to be doing your best work every time and taking every episode that they give you and make it the best it can possibly be. Then you can feel good about it and move on to the next one and do the same thing again.

And that applies even if you need to move a piece of the set ...

Yes, that's what you do. Do you play it in the booth? Do you play it up at the platform? Do you play it downstage? Do you play it at the counter? There are many options. The writing has specifically put you in certain places and they were right. But I had a place with that garbage can.... When Gary Wilde played by Brandon Johnson got out of that garbage can in Crusty's, that garbage can was never originally on the set. So, I placed the girls in proximity to the garbage can and placed the garbage can on the part of the set where I could shoot it.

Because you knew the show, that part of the set was ...

Barely seen. I made sure that the color of the garbage can was the same color as the other garbage can which has always been seen. I did everything I could to cheat the thing so that the fact is, it could have always been there but we didn't see it. I can do that because I have enough knowledge from how many times I shot scenes in that set to understand what I can get away with, what I can't get away with, what really doesn't matter, what I really need, proximity of staging to make things happen. Every once in a while, you take liberties because of its shootability. If I was around when this show was established, that couch would have never been of that angle to begin with. I would have

Step 2: Staging

gone to Greg, the designer, and said, "Are you out of your mind? They're sticking me in the coffin corner here. I can't get in there for the coverage as fast and efficiently as we need to get it."

Because the actors eyes are always looking upstage.

Yes. What's the difference? Just move it flat. Who cares? Because, once you're on the couch, it's just getting the best eyes. It's not about a visionary moment. I mean, it doesn't do that. Yes, every once in a while, you cheat. The funny thing about it is, nobody seems to mind my cheating. Nobody knows the difference anyway, half the time. I'm forever moving the kitchen table. Kitchen table has never been in the same place. The chairs, they wind up where I need them to be in every given scene. They change where I need them; if I need to lose a chair, fine. We move it over here. I can't have all four chairs at the table that seems to be in my way.

Then an important role of an assistant director is being able to see any voids in the master shots. If all your staging was upstage, then in the master shot I would roll in the butcher block table or the school bench depending on the set because it helped fill that ugly void at the bottom of the frame.

Yes. Certainly, they're called foreground cutting pieces. For the most part, it's a very useful tool, the foreground cutting piece. It's even more useful if, at some point, some people actually interact with this foreground cutting piece as opposed to just being a stationary piece of a table or a chair or something that just sits there. You have to make that determination of, when you're forced into a wide enough shot that you're really starting to feel like you're missing the foreground, you have put something into the foreground.

Staging: Applying the Learned Scene

Now you've addressed the sets according to the notes you made in the blue revised script and you've moved set pieces to accommodate any additional ideas you had from the writer's draft. So you've put some of the play on its feet.

Well, I've made sure that by this point whatever I put on its feet, it must

Staging: Applying the Learned Scene

be shoot-able. I know I wasn't putting anything on its feet that was going to be causing me major problems because you certainly don't want to be staging stuff and finding out there is no way to shoot it.

Like I've said earlier, you shoot sets, not actors, and you move actors to places on sets which give you the best-looking shots, the best variety of shots, the best whatever you're looking for, and we call this the best eyes—meaning you want to see two eyes on people, not just one eye on a profile. You want to see full faces if you can. So you do that kind of stuff and that night when I get my blue-paged script, I look it over, and I see all the changes they made.

The script has gotten tighter, it's gotten better. It maybe got shorter because it was too long at the table read and we know that our length of show is x-number of minutes and therefore we want to stay within the two- to three-minute range of that so that we have stuff to cut, but you're not looking to shoot episodes that are ten to fifteen minutes long.

We get a tighter script. I take a look at the changes. I see if the changes in the script will necessitate my re-staging stuff that I already did. I will think about the staging I did anyway and refine it. I consider the first time you put actors into a scene to do the scene, as the director's first draft; just like writers have a first draft. I have a first draft also.

I believe that staging actors gives them critical information. There are two sources of information that actors get. One is from the script, which they break down for themselves. They understand it emotionally. They understand the beats. They understand what's funny about it. If I need to help them, I will. A dialogue coach may help them. My goodness gracious, the hairdresser might help them for all I know, find something funny about something. They got that going.

What I've got to give them is the other piece of information they need to understand where the scene is going, that's how it's staged. How the scene moves. Why is it I decided to put one person on one end of the couch and the other person 15 feet away. Why did I do that? Why didn't I just have them sitting on the couch? I made that decision when I looked at the script, saying the scene plays better when they're further apart. Something about that scene told me, "Don't put them face to face, it's not what you want to do." Or certain scenes tell me that they have to be together. That's how you tell the story, in pictures, moving pictures.

Step 2: Staging

Is there a right way and a wrong way to do this?

No, I don't think so. Although there are people who have been accused, as directors, of not shooting the joke. That's an expression you hear all the time. Or confusing the story. If two actors are having an argument in a scene, it's one argument if we're across the room from each other. It's a decidedly different argument if we're in each other's faces. That has to be adjusted and thought about by the director. What kind of argument are you looking for? An in your face argument isn't the same as having an argument across the room. The screaming that can happen across a room and attacks are one thing, then having them next to each other, you can't do that.

Staging plays an important role.

A very important role in setting up another perimeter for what the actors have to deal with as they start to work their way through a scene to understand it fully, yes.

Emotionally.

Emotionally, yeah. Sometimes it helps them. If you stand on that line, I think it will help you, "Oh, yeah, you're right! That's much better." Or sometimes they'll just pop up from the couch by themselves and say, "I just felt I had to stand on this line," and 90 times out of 100 I'll say sure, because it really doesn't make that much difference to me, unless I really think they made a mistake.

If it's only half a dozen of one or six of the other, let the actor have it. Let the actor have it, give them that. Let them feel like they're inputting something and making a difference in their own performance. If it's that important to them to stand up, let them stand. But not until they have found the scene, until I understand that they know what the scene is about because I've studied the scene.

I guarantee you I've studied the scene a lot longer and a lot harder than the actors did. I pore over it and I look at it, and I understand it. I think of every permutation and combination of how that scene might play. Therefore, if somebody comes up to me and says, "What about…," I go, "I've already been through that in my brain, it ain't going to work. Because I'm going to have a problem over there." "Oh, yeah, you're right." That's the work you have to do.

Staging: The Physical Manifestation of the Story

Say Rocky in the series *Shake It Up* is coming through the window from the fire escape and CeCe, her best friend played by Bella Thorne, emotionally backs up and says, "Oh my God! This foreigner is coming after me!" In the episode Bella falls on her head and gets amnesia and forgets who Rocky is but I never told her to do that. I never said anything. I just let them do what they were going to do as actors. What am I supposed to say, "Now Bella, as soon as she comes in the window, you don't know who she is, and you're scared of her."? She's going to do that instinctively and I want to get her instincts going in the scene.

It wound up being a very good choice that she made and it made the scene a better scene because she let the moment come from a real place for her which also affected the physical blocking of the scene. But that's ok, as the director I knew the actor brought something to the scene that I couldn't explain. Only she could bring what she truly felt inside.

Yes, but in reference to the staging, you placed them by the window.

Oh, setting it up, yes. I understand I set that up so that if she made the choice, she wound up making the right choice. I understand that completely. That's why I put her mother, Anita Barone, behind the counter when Rocky came through the window. This way the mother can open it up; it was to make that thing between Rocky and CeCe happen. Is there another way to do it? Probably, but that was not the way I saw it. The way I saw it is the way I staged it and it worked for the actors and we produced a good scene out of it.

So now this is where going to the set before you even begin your production meeting to learn the sets ...

Is critical.

Staging: The Physical Manifestation of the Story

How did staging become your starting point?

The ability to work with actors in no way informs your ability to visualize camerawork. They are two parts of the brain that are not necessarily in the same place. The fact that I had both of those skills was unique for me to be able to make it work for sitcom. I was a stage manager in theater. I would do

Step 2: Staging

big musicals where I'd have to call 350 cues in the course of an act in *Carousel* with Robert Goulet and Carol Lawrence out there, and I'm backstage going, "Light 73 go, lights 82 go, sound 47 go," and I'm going like that so I had a technical understanding of how you must hold on to that information. It became easier for me with my background being primarily in working with actors to working with cameras because I had a mind that was not outrageously foreign to that. I was able to absorb it quickly. My skill set worked for me in this arena, that's all.

So your work with actors helped you to recognize the importance of staging.

Very much so. I taught acting for many years, and I taught the principles of a guy who ran the Polish Lab Theater named Jerzy Grotowski. Grotowski was the first person to come out with an acting book that was not based on Stanislavski's method. It was based on other things. His concept was that you trained an actor as if he were an athlete. It was the body and the physical that informed the emotional. It was Reiki-an in a sense as opposed to Freudian.

The Grotowski method was that physical posturing will inform emotion as to what is going on in the body. You can feed it the other way around. Essentially, that's what staging is. Staging is the physical manifestation of the story, and that is critical, and if I stage it right, it will feed the actor into the attitudes and into the emotions, and into the sense of everything that I need and if I hadn't done it right, I'd have to go home, I'd have to do my homework and say, "What about the structure that I set up is hanging them up?"

I've got to re-think a little bit my next draft of my staging to get more specific because right now I seem to be not quite getting it done in spots. I'll go home and do my homework again, refining my script; which is my staging. I refine my staging just like the writers are refining their writing, and hopefully, we'll come to the same place at the same time.

Now, once again, I'm talking here from the point of view of someone with many, many years of experience and what writers will allow me to input that they might not allow a beginner to input. But I'll forever go to Rob Lotterstein and Rob will say, "Oh, maybe I should get rid of this." I'll say, "Rob, that's a good scene. Give me one more day with it. Leave it alone." And he'll trust me to give it one more day. I'm not sure that another director who was doing the

Staging: The Physical Manifestation of the Story

first or second episode on that show could go and say that to him if you can't prove it to him. But I know I can prove it to him. For example, that insane little scene where we determined that we were going to put Flynn played by Davis Cleveland into a locker at CeCe's school. Rob kept saying, "Wow. I think we got to get rid of this bit. It's stupid that he's in the locker." I said, "I think I can make it work. Give me one more day with it. Don't mess with the scene." He gave me the day and we made it work. Not only did we make it work, we made it work so well, he stuck Anita Barone in that locker for the tag.

That was something that I saw in my brain. I knew that was going to work. I couldn't show it to them at the first run-through because … I couldn't quite get him into that locker. I didn't have any of that world to sell, which I knew I could get the next day.

So sometimes I would beg for him to leave a scene alone, "I think you wrote it beautifully. Don't mess with the scene. I got some adjustments to do. Let me take my adjustments." Nine times out of ten, they'll give me that. Every once in a while, they'll go back and say, "No, I know he thinks he can do it, but we got a better idea. Let's get rid of it now. Let's not deal with it." They'll make their writing choices and I'll deal with that.

That's why staging is so important, because you go with the method of the physicality of the actor to bring out their emotions.

That's right.

Ironically enough, that's where we're in sync because that's how I work. I was able to funnel my sense of direction into the show which you prepped, you prepped right there on stage. I'm going to school. I'm watching the teacher. I'm getting paid to go to school here, but this is now a form that I know I'm going to thrive in …

Oh, yeah.

… because we speak the same language. I will always stage first.

Yeah. I'm a "stage firster," always have been. That's what I do. I believe in it. It works in most situations. Actors really don't want to spend time staging themselves. These guys do one show a week. They're not interested in inventing. Once in a while, you have a Bronson Pinchot, who was an inventor on

Step 2: Staging

Perfect Strangers. He was always trying to find something new and something different and something ... outrageously something or other in everything we were doing. But Mark and I used to keep him under control. It took both of us working him to keep him under control. The great classic thing about Bronson was, we're about to do a scene, and he comes storming in. He says, "Okay, I'm going to come in from the door. I'm going to cross to the kitchen. I will grab myself a drink. I will sit at the bar. I would do that, that, that. Then I would cross to the couch." I said, "Bronson, that's terrific staging. However, as your director, I need to inform you that, at that moment, all the cameras will be pointed at the couch." He went, "Oh, in that case I'll come in. I'll sit on the couch and we'll do the scene."

I said, "That's an excellent choice, Bronson." [*Laughs*] "Of course, then you'll be on camera." You play the game in terms of how that's done, but for the most part, I think actors appreciate getting as much information as possible. Then they can start to make some creative decisions on their own.

Funny lines will work, but the difference in making them better is in the timing and in the physical placement of the actors.

Very much so. The other thing adding to that is that every actor has their own sense of timing and what might be a funny timing for you that you think would be the best ... or the writer, for that matter ... was not in the actor's natural rhythm. I was talking to Chris Thompson about that. He said, "The beautiful thing about Tom Hanks was that he never ever spoke the rhythms that the writers thought he should speak. He always found something that was funnier." It would just blow our minds. He used to have bends on lines that nobody was expecting. Yet they were self-fulfilled.

Chris wrote for Bosom Buddies?

He created it.

I didn't know that.

Yes. That's where Kris Trexler, the editor on *Shake It Up*, Chris Thompson the creator of *Shake It Up*, me, all of us come together from *Bosom Buddies*. Kris Trexler was the editor on *Bosom Buddies*. We go back to that particular period of time together. I've done a lot of these buddy comedies, *Laverne &*

Staging: The Physical Manifestation of the Story

Shirley, Bosom Buddies and then *Perfect Strangers* and now *Shake It Up*. Each one, they're all honed the same way, but the organic thing that happens is completely different because they're different human beings. They just play differently. They have different timings between them.

But with buddy comedies, you also have the straight person with the funny actor.

Usually, buddies …

Once you knew the physical comedy that an actor was capable of, then how would you stage that in your mind? How would that help you as a director?

First of all, it's a question of how close you can shoot them. If they are very physical, you can't shoot them very closely. You'll be missing out on all the funny things that they're doing with their arms, with their bellies or whatever else it is. You have to shoot them a certain way, that's for sure. Also, they take over. If they have an inkling or bend on something physical, they will always explode with it before you get to say a word about it. Then all you're doing is helping them shape it. Of course, if you have an instrument that you're playing that has enormous skills as a physical comic, well, you're playing a Stradivarius at that point.

Then the work that you get to do is so much more elevated because you got a man or a woman who is capable of some outrageous physical things. Cindy Williams is one of the best physical actresses I've ever seen. She was funny. She was gutsy. She went out on a limb and did things that I would not believe that an actress would even want to do. She was remarkable at that. She was a physical actress. Penny Marshall was much more of the straight man, a little oversexed, but the funny one was the prude. The prude is the one who would fall into pits and fall into things and do all the physical stuff. Can you even do that?

Even like in The Odd Couple.

Same thing. All buddy comedy has somebody who reacts while somebody is being funny, and that's what you need. I think that Bronson Pinchot loved Mark Linn-Baker because he knew that whatever stupidity he came up with, when he turned around, there would be Mark Linn-Baker staring at him. He always knew that Mark was going to be there.

Disciplining the Physical Excesses of an Actor

How did that help you stage an actor who brings a physical presence to a character?
You have a core that puts you in a place that the other person can then go spinning around because they're always going to get back to the core. The core doesn't leave. It's not a question of staging. It's disciplining the excesses, meaning if you've got an actor who will go out of the box physically, your job then is to control it enough that it stays within the parameters of the world of the show that we're doing, that it stays within the character representation that's not so far outside the world that we lose it.

Let's take a look at the great example of Kramer. Kramer was created as a physical character on *Seinfeld*. He wasn't doing many verbal jokes. They didn't write him verbal jokes. They've had him walk into a wall. They had him falling down. He had all kinds of physical mannerisms, but he was a phenomenally gifted physical actor. They built that role for him. That was what that role was going to be all about. He was just going to be a physical chameleon. When you get an actor with that level of skill, you try to use it, like when we found out that Bronson and Mark could do physical comedy together that was quite astonishing. They could break into dances. They could sing and they could do all kinds of stuff. We started to utilize it.

But for staging purposes when one of these physically brilliant actors was in a scene, then whatever props or tools, props being a door, props being a refrigerator, props being whatever—the couch, the table, whatever they were falling over, whatever they were running into—then that dictated to you where you were staging a scene.
Yes, very much so, but then again, where you stage your scene is up for grabs in a number of places. The script will say "Living Room" or it will say "CeCe's Living Room." I'll look at the script and I'll go, "Wait a second. They got four scenes in CeCe's Living Room in this episode. I got to do something

here. I have to think, is there any one of these scenes I can play in the kitchen? How can I break this up?" Because when you direct enough, you begin to realize the most boring space to stage a scene is in the living room, because the only thing that can happen in the living room is talking or watching the TV, unless somebody's going to bring in an activity from the kitchen.

Well, why not do it in the kitchen if they're going to bring in the activity anyway? Unless they're sitting there at the couch doing their homework, they're all passive activities. You either watch TV, you sit on a couch, you do homework, you nibble on something or other, but it's all passive. There's no physical activity. Move them into a kitchen, and all of a sudden you got people who are getting a snack from the refrigerator. There's all kinds of movement that's more natural. You'll look for it and you'll break down the script and say, "Oh, boy. Too many scenes in the living room." You'll go to the producer and say, "I'm going to move this scene into the kitchen, if it's okay with you." The writers have been asking me lately where I'm playing scenes. They just assume that I will find a balance of scenes so that it's not all in the same place, because it is very hard to make it look different if it's all in the same place.

So, yes, that becomes a real responsibility where the scene is taking place and therefore what activities that space allows you and what kind of staging opportunities that space allows you as opposed to a living room or a bedroom.

Step 3: Dialogue

Day 2: Engaging the Actors

Positioning the actors in relation to each other to best express the dialogue is the focus of this chapter. Joel's process starts to take shape here because he has set up a foundation that makes working with the dialogue not only stronger but also easier. Step 3 is very important because the writers really don't care as much about the blocking of actors compared to hearing the dialogue they've written come to life. They want to witness the efficacy of their words. Dialogue is the driving force that, if delivered effectively, will reinforce the writer's intentions. If people laugh, then the writers know they have succeeded.

The Importance of Dialogue

Now we're at Step 3, still rehearsal day, still in the blue revised table draft. Give me a description of the importance of dialogue in a situation comedy.

A situation comedy is driven 95 percent by dialogue. You might have some physical aspects to a show, which we used to call the block scene or the big events scene where I don't know what that could be. In *Family Matters*, we actually had a tornado go off in the kitchen. That's a block scene. We have had scenes on *Shake It Up* that are decidedly block scenes in nature, somebody in a cleaning place riding on one of those dry cleaning garment conveyors. Events that occur that are blocked tend to be physical, but for the most part 95 percent of the episode is driven by the attempt to tell the story through dialogue. Dialogue becomes important because we have different ways of operating with dialogue. There are producers, and it's the producer's medium we talked about that, who basically want to hear the exact dialogue they wrote come back from the actors mouths when they come down to see a run-through. And as a director, you better give them what they expect to hear. There have been many shows I've been on where that was not necessarily the course of events. Buddy comedy (as I did with *Laverne & Shirley, Bosom Buddies and Perfect Strangers*) necessitates a certain amount of byplay between the buddies and you will find that there is more inventiveness allowed by the producers on the floor in terms of sprucing up dialogue or perhaps removing a line or perhaps adding a line that makes sense because you're trying to put together a scene and it's necessary to allow some freedom on the stage to slightly improvise dialogue.

My warning to actors doing that was that if you come up with a very simple fix for a problem that you think you're having and it's specific, you got it. However, you cannot give me a generalized answer. If you can't be more specific than the script, then just do what the script says. That's always been my general rule of thumb concerning ad libs. If you come up with something very sharp and very spiffy and I'm in a situation where the producers are actually wanting that kind of inventiveness on the set, go for it. Other than that, give the producers what they wrote and let them determine whether or not they need to rewrite or fix or make the joke cleaner or make the joke hotter. Yes, the dialogue is the driving force of sitcom.

Also, if there's questions that can't be answered on the set, the normal procedure is to call up to the writers room.

If I have the time I'll call up and I'll say, "Have the executive producer come down to the stage as soon as he comes in. Let him know I got a real problem with the beginning of a scene and I want to speak to him about it before I have to worry about getting it ready for a run-through for him or for anybody." That will happen and the executive producer will stop by the set. I'll say what the problem is and he'll go, "Oh, yeah, okay, well, then let's do it this way." He will give me a quick fix on the problem and we'll get it up on its feet with that quick fix in, so that he can see it and I can move ahead with my day without being completely hamstrung by a sequence that's not making any sense.

Step 3: Dialogue

And if you don't have the time, you usually have the script supervisor flag the moment.

Yes, the script supervisor will flag anything we find problematical on the stage. She will also make any kind of small modifications we might make in dialogue in order to send that script up to the writers room, so when they're doing their rewrite on Tuesday night and getting ready for the next version, they've got the stage notes as they call them. And they can determine based on the stage notes and the other work they're doing whether they think what we've come up with is better than what they had or they need something completely different.

Pacing and Cues and Acting Styles

Comedy often relies on word play because it sets words and phrases in a specific order to capitalize on a laugh. Now, how do you feel about the pacing of the dialogue while you're rehearsing?

Usually comedy moves at a pretty rapid pace. There are scenes which are more dramatic than comedic, where time must be taken by the actors in terms of making the moments real. Usually, if you're having trouble with the scene, you might ask the actors to do it a little faster and nine times out of ten that will solve the problem. They're just playing it too slow and the innate rhythms that make something funny aren't coming across because they're too lugubrious at that point.

I'm not saying that's a suggestion that you make every time but, usually, picking up cues is so important to pacing. Then if you want to take a little time delivering your line because of something you're trying to make happen, that's fine and dandy. The death of comedy is simply not picking up cues. You've got to pick up your cues.

Describe cues.

One person finishes speaking and the other person starts speaking. For example, if Actor 1 says, "I think we should go out Saturday night," you're supposed to say, "No, I don't think we should go out Saturday night." She says, "Why do you think we should not go out Saturday night? We always go out

Saturday night." "Well, this Saturday night I got...," etc. If you take pauses in between those lines, that entire argument is out the window. Obviously you have to deal with that specifically within the script but, as a rule of thumb, dropping cues is a key thing that can destroy comedy.

While we're on that subject, do you ever come across actors who have been trained in a specific style and has that been an advantage or a disadvantage or both?

I would tend to think that every actor I work with has been trained in a different style or not trained at all. The job of the director is to somehow create an environment where all these people with their disparate language, in terms of how they work, can still operate. Because, to be quite honest, when you're in a professional world and you're being paid a pretty nice salary to perform a role that people are very excited about you performing, we're not interested in your process. Couldn't care less what the actor's process is. Whether he's trained with Meisner, whether he actually trained at the Actor's Studio, with Uta Hagen, or whether he came from standup comedy, or Lee Strasberg, or whether he worked with the Second City, or maybe, an improvisational group, like "Off the Wall," which Robin Williams came out of, basically it's not important to me how they get to things. The only thing that's important to me is that they get there. Now, if the actor specifically, because of their own orientation, has a problem and they wish to speak to me about their problem, I will engage in that discussion always, always will give the actor his due if the actor has a real problem with what they're trying to do.

I did a directing forum over at the Geffen Theater recently with five pretty major directors including Taylor Hackford and a couple other people and we tried to discuss what directing was. What the hell do you do for directing? What is it about? The remarkable thing was, all five of us had the exact same opinion of what directing was and that blew my mind because we come from different places. I'm a freak from La MaMa on the Lower East Side doing experimental theater and Taylor Hackford had just won the Academy Award for *Ray*. The other guy ran the Geffen and somebody else ran theaters. And Randall Arney, who runs the Geffen Theater, had the best visual I've ever heard about this thing. He said, "When I get into a situation, I basically come in and I place a cone, a metaphorical cone over each actor. I will not go into that cone unless the actor invites me in, however; I will move that cone, staging it, wherever I think that cone should be in order to give the actor the best chance to understand the flow and the desires of a given scene."

It's the same thing we were talking about. He said, "Once the actor basically starts to work, I move these pieces, these cones, they're almost like chess pieces around a board. Now the actor starts to input once they understand the language they're supposed to speak, follow the staging they're supposed to do. Now you may get input from the actor, at that point the actor will let you into his little cone and you can solve a problem with an actor." He said he would never go into an actor's cone unless asked in. Which I thought was very interesting. I just sat there and went, "Far out" I said, "Randall, boy, you hit it. You found the image that really is true."

Rules of Comedy and Directing Actors

Are there any general rules for making comedy work in dialogue?
There have been standard comedy rules for a long time that comedic timing works in threes. Anything with the letter K in it tends to be funny. There's rhythms to things that basically may have no meaning and just the rhythm itself is funny. They've been around for years, it's not a discussion. The biggest discussion, to be quite honest, because there's no way to teach this, they don't teach it in college, they don't teach it any place, how do you direct actors? What do you do with these people? These are a strange bunch of people, actors. They have egos. They have neuroses. That's probably the reason they're such great actors: because they've got all that going. You need an enormous ego to survive an industry which is constantly telling you that you suck. You just have to have ego. How do you deal with that? How do you direct actors? What is that skill all about?

Everybody comes to that stylistically differently, they really do. Some people believe they can teach acting. I don't believe that. I don't believe that the proper place to teach acting is in a work arena where people are being paid a lot of money because theoretically they can act. My thing is to stimulate them to challenge themselves, to question choices that they make and encourage them. "You know, that was a brilliant choice. Why don't we push it one step further?" I'm not going to sit there and ever give a line reading to an actor or will I ever suggest the rhythm. I might suggest, "Pick up your cues." I might suggest, "You're talking too low, I can't hear you, you can't be funny if I can't hear you." I might suggest that you need to talk faster or slower or I couldn't even make out the words. The fact is, I'm not about teaching acting.

I taught acting for five, six years. Taught at Yale School of Drama, taught at Queens College, Wheaton College, Brooklyn College, I've taught at Kent State. I taught acting but you don't teach professional actors. In my estimation, if they're not good enough, they shouldn't have been hired. I do believe that you stimulate them. I do believe that you energize them. I do believe you want to find out what they do best and help them do it.

Earlier I was talking about Chris Thompson because to add to all of this, Tom Hanks was essentially his muse. He felt that Tom was the voice, the comic voice that was truly coming out of him. He always thought that even though Tom had rhythms that were decidedly not Chris'. He had a sense of rhythm about how he did these lines that was so idiosyncratic. It was so his own. There was nothing predictable about his reading. He just had a style that he was so cocky with, was so self-assured with. That's what he did best. That was quite amazing, considering he had no reason to be self-assured. His experience level was minimal. Yet, he just knew that he had to be him. He understood that about himself.

I have another anecdote about this girl. We're doing this pilot, it was a buddy comedy, it was two girls and I think they were trying at that time to find something that could replace *Laverne & Shirley* kind of humor. They were constantly trying to find two girls. Put them together and see if magic happened. I went to the set and we did the producer run-through. We're now going into the third day and I finally had to go up to this girl and I actually said to her, "Excuse me, dear. What is it that you do?" And she asked, "What do you mean?"

I said, "What is it that you do? I've been watching now for two days and you're not doing anything. You're sitting when I tell you to sit. You're crossing when I tell you to cross. You're saying the lines that are in the script but you're not doing anything. Why did they hire you? What was it they saw in you that you're not showing me? I can't help you if I don't know what it is you're capable of doing."

Step 3: Dialogue

My style with actors has always been to encourage them to do what they think is the best possible thing they can do and then I will help shape them at that point or encourage them at that point or cajole them at that point. I might even jokingly embarrass them because they blew a moment so substantially that it was wonderful to watch. Diving off that high board and not realizing there was no water in the pool is a wonderful thing and if we can all embrace the insanity of actors trying to make reality work out of a piece of writing, I find that that's my best skill. Whereas other people want to try to teach acting, and I'm not so sure that actors who are professionals want to be taught.

Yes, some people can get away with it. You have to have a real easygoing style to find a way to encourage an actor to act. Like with *Shake It Up*, I decided to find out what Zendaya and Bella were made of. I just made them find the scenes by themselves and, you know something?, little by little they got better and better and better and all of a sudden they're finding 90, 95 percent of the scenes by themselves with no help from anybody. I don't think that would happen if I was nursing and I'm feeding them line by line what I thought the truth should be. I only have to talk to them if they're really off in left field on something and that would be like, "What are you doing, my dear? Exactly what was that moment about?"

I make them explain to me what their thought process was and I found out to my amazement, with *Shake It Up*, the girls had a decided process they were going on. They really did think about that. I'm like, "Wow, they really think about this." Sometimes with teenagers, you think they're not thinking about anything. But they really did, they said, "Oh, no, I don't feel I should say the line that way because I feel that if I do it that way I'm demeaning the other character and I don't think my character should demean the other character." I'm going, "You're right, she shouldn't demean the other character," and we can come to an understanding of what's going on. They surprise you.

Child actors come from a place of innocence. They can bring more to the table than adult actors because they're not tainted, not affected.

They don't have much ego, so therefore they have less baggage. If you can allow them to be the kids they're supposed to be. I grew Mary-Kate and Ashley Olsen up from six months old to eight years old. I had Jodie Sweetin.

I had Candace Cameron. Now I have Zendaya and Bella Thorne. I lived through the Urkel phenomenon on *Family Matters*, and all the kids on *Step by Step*. The interesting thing about it is, if you can let them be kids and let them make the judgments that they feel are honest for themselves, you can get some remarkable things out of these kids. It's truly amazing because there's no pretense. They haven't gotten to a place of pretending yet, they're just doing it. If the adults could learn something from watching kids, just do it. They're not thinking about it. Whatever homework they've done is their own business. They're not interested in telling you that they've thought this through. They're just going to go out and do it. I enjoy that, I really do. That's why I love working with kids.

But I Didn't Study Acting ...

What advice would you give to directors who may not have studied acting before coming on to direct a situation comedy?

I'm not sure it hurts them. Their vocabulary must be in how to encourage actors, to stimulate actors, to cajole actors, to work them, to play with them, and to holler at them. They're not going to be able to teach. They're not going to be able to do that. Yes, you come to a show where the actors can do most of it for you and it's not needed, then you're okay.

You get on a show where the director needs to be an energy source for the show; has to be the center of energy. The energy is going to either come from the director or everything is going to lie flat there. You're the choir leader, baby, as a director. You've got to set the tone, set the energy level, set the pace that you want this work done at. That's part of the system that exists anywhere because you don't have an unlimited amount of time to do this work. You find a way of getting shorthand with the actors. That's why many producers do like to have one director who's on the floor; who becomes their muse, so to speak. Really gives them what it is their vision is or least its amalgamated vision between the director and the writers, the performers, producers. It all becomes a mix at some particular point; with a political pecking order that must be paid attention to. It's a writing medium and you better let the writers have their head, otherwise you're going to have the door.

Step 3: Dialogue

Sense of Humor

You mentioned how you need to be the center of energy. Explain how incorporating your sense of humor into the process is a big part of that energy.

As the director in a sitcom, you are the first audience the actors get. If you're not responding to what they're doing, it just dies. You have to be the kind of a person who finds funny in things that are happening even though you know it can get funnier. It's not your job to get worried about that now. If it's funny enough, laugh. Enjoy yourself. You're there to have a good time. Situation comedy is the best job in the world. You're going to laugh all day long. You want to laugh at what they're doing even though you know it will be better and it will be funnier.

You have to stick with the process. Today, it's this, tomorrow it will be better, next day will be better and then by the time you shoot it, that's where it's got to be the best it's going to be during the course of the week. You have to trust the process. I believe the director has to trust the process because the producers, they hear things in their head from the day they write it. They're much more result-oriented than the director tends to be. They expect to see what they wrote the first time that they get to see it, where the director knows that this is the first. We're going to move along, just keep the process going. We'll get better.

They'll take a rewrite. We'll work the rewrite. It will be funnier. We'll work the rewrite. It will be more touching, but essentially we believe in process. If you believe that your process is a healthy process and you believe that I know for myself that I've now proven to myself countless times that if I keep the process pure, I will always get the best possible result. Always get the best possible result.

What do you mean by "keep the process pure"?

It's based on your own sense of humor, it's based on your own sensibility towards the actors around you and how you respond to that. It's based on stuff in the writing that you think is brilliant. I've had writers decide that no, no, no, that's not working, and I would go over to them and I'd say, "Give me another shot with this thing. This is brilliant writing and I'm not going to let you give up this writing because it didn't happen on the first day of rehearsal. I will make this work. I believe in this writing."

STEP 4: FINE TUNING THE ACTING

Day 2: The Tools of the Craft

Positioning the actors in relation to each other for ease of shooting is an important part of staging, and requires an instinct of how to incorporate movement, body language and props into a scene. There is a subliminal aspect to directing. In this chapter, Joel shares tips for tapping into the show's energy that will help create and maintain the proper flow. Creating the building blocks up to this point enables a director to move through the process more efficiently.

Time Management

Sometimes you've got ten minutes to rehearse scenes. How do you know which scenes demand less rehearsal time?
It took me years to realize that it's all about the writing. You give me good writing and actors who know what they're doing and literally, it's a vacation week. You don't have any work to do, you really don't. If you're starting to pick away at stuff that's beautifully well-written, you're a fool. You've just got to accept the scenes that are just happening,

I've got Adam Irigoyen playing Deuce and Ainsley Bailey playing Dina in *Shake It Up* over at the counter and Deuce wants to grow a moustache. The scene is hysterically written. The actors have found it in five seconds flat. For me to beat that to death is crazy. That's it, you did it once, get out of here. Figure it out for the run-through, you got this, you know this one. I'll do that with virtually any scene that I think is a lock. These people know it, they know

Step 4: Fine Tuning the Acting

the humanity of the scene, and they know the funny of the scene. The writers have written a gorgeous scene. I just leave it alone.

I have to work on the scenes that are perhaps a little more complicated in terms of staging. I have to save time if there's a bloody scene where we're going to hang somebody from a clock, or whatever the craziness comes in when you're doing physical comedy for kids. I have to save time for that and working with you; you tend to know that's what's going to happen and you make sure that I save time for the big babies. The little fish can be thrown in and let them grow up at the run-through as they need to because the writing is there.

Then how do you deal with the actor who says, "I still need to work this out in my head. I need to spend more time on it," when you know you don't have the time?

I don't indulge that, as you know [*laughs*]. In a sitcom you cannot, if it's that complicated in your head that you can't figure it out, you're in the wrong business. The writing for sitcom has to be basically pretty much on the surface. We're not talking about great motivational reasons. We're not talking about all that. You have to stay pretty surfacey; otherwise it isn't going to be funny. Therefore, if an actor's having trouble, if it's about the writing my answer is, "I can't fix that for you right now. The writers will be sent a note saying you've got a problem in this area." I'll do that. I'll write a note down for that but right now for us to take time to try to solve your problem, when I think the problem needs to be solved by the writers, is a waste of our time.

I would certainly be pleasant about that. The fact is, it's a writing problem. If you're having this much trouble in a sitcom, playing a role that you played for three years, with a line, let's let them rewrite the line. That's really the way to deal with that. You can't get into that because you're not on the floor rewriting for them.

The Importance of Props

How did you learn about the relationship between actors and props?

Interesting, I trained on *Laverne & Shirley*. I spent two years on that show in the beginning of my career. Penny and Cindy took me to school in terms of how a scene is structured physically. When we could finally get them out of their dressing rooms [*laughs*], Penny would come out and say, "Okay, all right, I see the scene here. I'm going to have my pocketbook on this table. I would like my jacket on that chair. I would like to make sure that there's a milk and Pepsi in the refrigerator, and now I also need an umbrella in the umbrella stand. Okay, Joel, call action." Action! She would cross over, she'd get her pocketbook. She'd pick up her pocketbook. She'd cross, she'd get her wallet out and while the dialogue was going on, she'd know exactly when to cross because she made sure you don't cross on a punchline but after it. Then she'd get to the next place and go to her milk and Pepsi. Pour that, have a drink of that. Head out, grab her coat, grab her umbrella and she's out the door. The whole thing is staged based on activity that she knew she needed to get out the door. That she needed to carry herself through the scene. Some of it involved props but it was more a sense of the activity of a scene that is really important.

If the activity of a scene is simply people leaving the room; they're getting ready to go and then they go. Then there are certain activities that you can give them if you choose to. Put on a coat, take off a coat. Usually with younger kids, they don't tend to be caring that much about props and about activity.

To help facilitate the comedy.

Indeed. Interestingly enough, I worked with an actress who's a great prop actress, she will never enter the bloody room without her keys. At the front door, she has the keys, opens the lock because the whole point is that you can't have kids in an apartment without the door being locked. If there's no knock on the door, she has keys, but nobody else has keys. Unless there's a specific moment where they must have keys for something that the script has called for, they don't worry about that particular thing. "Ah, who cares, I'll just come in. They'll think that I did it on the outside." They'll assume that I turned the key. Not with this actress. She turns the key.

Sometimes actors can help bring something to the rehearsal.

You bet. That's one of the things that the director has to do. When you do your staging, your staging is about a flow of activity that takes the actors from the couch to the kitchen to the refrigerator, to the counter, back to the couch, out a window—whatever that staging is about. If you need a motivation for staging, now that's sometimes where props come in. I have a scene and I feel like the scene's got to move. This is contrary to what I said to Bronson where his staging of himself was going to get in the way of the scene.

Now, I've got CeCe on the phone and her mother is listening into this stupid conversation about the fact that she wants a limo for her Sweet 16 party. Finally she picks up the phone, puts it down and I have her cross down to the table where the remains of her lunch are sitting. That was just me, because I knew I had a reason to cross over to the table to pick up this plate which she had been eating off of. Take this plate to the sink and then come back and finish this scene. It gave me just enough motivated activity and movement to construct a pattern of how I wanted that scene to flow. I knew that if I kept that scene stagnant in one place, it was going to die. I had to have reasons why they were going any place.

Props also help you accentuate some of the dialogue in comedy.

And the places where the jokes come in. There's no question about it. Props help set up the joke. By getting them to the place where they have to be, and not forcing them to stand there all the time waiting to deliver a joke.

Lines, Movement and Placement

For the most part, there are rules about delivering lines. You mentioned Penny Marshall and how she didn't cross on a punchline but after it.

You do physical action on your own line. You don't do physical action on somebody else's line. At that point, I may be on a close-up with that person doing their line and not on the physical action you're doing, so you're wasting your time. All of a sudden you've jumped on me. You're forcing me to include you in a shot that I may not want to include you in. So the rule of thumb is, you move on your own lines and you don't move on somebody else's line. Very simple.

I think that can hold true 98 percent of the time; unless you want to shoot them in a two-shot. Therefore, it's nice while one person is carrying on, if the other person decides to plop down on the couch disgruntled, you could do that. Certainly it will happen but essentially the rule tends to be "Move on your own lines not on somebody else's line." You don't want to move on a joke. You want to be able to hit the punchline of a joke. Everybody knows what the punchline is and then after the punchline, while people are laughing, if you wish to make a move, you then make a move to some other thing. An activity that you want to continue doing, or plop in a chair and pick up your computer, any of those choices of naturalistic activity, but you don't walk on a joke line.

That's specifically for the comedy but also for camera.

We are trying to get the best visual for this little movie that we're making each week that's a modified proscenium kind of a shoot. We want to get the most visual. Therefore, when people have the funniest lines, we want to have the best shots of their face when they're going to deliver that line. That seems to be something that everybody seems to want. There may be a gag somewhere that may be funnier because the person's back is to the camera. I'm not suggesting that wouldn't be a possibility, but that's a unique thing that would depend upon a specific thing that the script is trying to accomplish.

For the most part you're driven by dialogue and driven by jokes, because the nature of sitcom is jokey. That's why the ones with the laugh track are jokier than the ones without a laugh track like *The Office* or *30 Rock*. They're not as jokey. They don't go for jokes that get you laughs. They make you do character things that are amusing but sitcom, *Two and a Half Men*, *The Nerd Show*, are very much into into character. Character and funny jokes, funny lines, funny attitudes, and these people stay put for those funny lines and funny attitudes. Every once in a while I suppose you might get caught as a director and you have no choice but to cross somebody on a joke. That better not be more than two percent of the time, otherwise they're not going to be happy with you.

In theater, you have actors who need to project to be heard in the back row of the theater. How do you work on the television set in order to get the most out of the dialogue?

That's very much a question of a personal choice and a matter of time. If you're going to put yourself in a corner of the set, which necessitates more shooting time just simply to cover it that has nothing to do with performance value, you can't do that to yourself too often because it just eats up too much

Step 4: Fine Tuning the Acting

time. In the final analysis it doesn't make that much of a difference. You want to get dialogue; you want to be able to see faces with dialogue. You want to be able to see relationships. You want to be able to tell the story with your camerawork. Sticking things into corners of sets that might be visually interesting to do … you're taking up much too much time. It's something you really have to think about.

Do you have the time? I know we play games at Crusty's. I'll move them into a booth way upstage which necessitates an awful lot of schlepping around and moving to get to the shot. We know my pace and we know I can accomplish that. Even then I try to take a balance of how many times I want to go there. How much time will that eat up just by camera movement? Having to go deeper into the set to shoot?

The further away you are from the back of the set, the better it looks. The more you press yourself up against fake backdrops that are supposed to be the City of Chicago, the less real it looks. You tend to want to bring people away from the back of the stage as much as possible and it's easier to shoot them when they're further down stage.

Theater has a system of directions which are based on an actor's point of view. Stage right is the actor's right as he's facing the audience. Stage left is the actor's left as he's facing the audience. Upstage is moving away from the audience and downstage is moving toward the audience. Those are the basics and then from that point on you can make it work. However, it's exactly the reverse in film or on camera. Now it's the camera point of view. Camera left is the cameraman's left. Camera right is the cameraman's right. Upstage is still upstage although film actors don't know that term. It always throws them. What do I mean by upstage? It means further away from the camera and downstage means coming closer to the cameras. One of the things with any system and the ability to move fast for the system is vocabulary. You have to have vocabulary for all these choices that is very fast and very specific. Then everybody starts to understand the vocabulary and shorthand develops so that all of a sudden things are moving twice as fast as it did before.

That's probably one of the reasons why I can move as fast as I do; because I know how to speak. I have vocabulary to camera operators, and I have vocabulary to actors that are shorthand ways of getting what I need done in a specific amount of time.

Step 5: Writers' and Producers' Run-Through

Day 2: Final Preparation

This chapter covers how the writers' and producers' run-through is essential in finding what works and what doesn't so that the play stands a chance of being the best it can be by the end of Day 5. This run-through is a litmus test. Joel describes how he handles the positive and negative responses to the director's vision. Sometimes the presentation may not have all of the desired elements in place, whether a guest cast actor is not working yet, or certain props or special effects are still in the building phase, or a wardrobe gag still in the works. There are often many incidentals that have yet to be incorporated. However, it's the next step in the collaborative effort that helps the process to continue on the right track. This step is based on a mutual understanding that the script is still a work in progress.

Writer-Producer Run-Through

Let's talk about the first test in showing your work to the writers and producers in the form of a run-through.

I got the revised script on Monday night. I've gone through it very specifically to see what changes they came up with and how that would affect any staging I already did or any staging I need to do. Then I go in, and the AD has a schedule worked out for me as to what time I will be doing what scene with who based on his own knowledge of what it is that's got to be done, and I basically go to work, staying within the time frame that's been created for me of how fast and how efficiently these scenes must be put on their feet,

Step 5: Writers' and Producers' Run-Through

so that by the time we get ready for an afternoon run-through, this whole little 23-minute play has been staged, the actors have gotten to do it. They feel comfortable enough with what they're doing to be able to do the run-through, the dreaded run-through for the producers who come down *en masse* with their whole staff of writers and some other technical people, mothers and fathers show up and all kinds of strange people, and we do this producer run-through.

Each producer has a different style of doing run-throughs. Some basically let the whole show runthrough; they then give the notes to the director who gives the notes to the actors the next day that they meet. Some like to give the notes to the actors themselves, which is against DGA [Directors Guild of America] rules, but it doesn't bother me one way or the other. I think that producers have a right to be able to speak to actors and to be able to ask actors for certain things that they didn't think they were getting. I think that's just fine. I sometimes have to go over to the actor after a producer note and tell them, "Ignore it, it'll drive you nuts. Forget about it, I'll clarify it for you tomorrow." Other than that, let them do whatever they do.

Then the writers will go back up into their room and they will do their next set of revisions. I will get that set of revisions, now on Tuesday night. I think you call them the pinks at that point.

Now what happens is that everything up to that point is either approved or not by the executive producer. And notes are given to make changes not just to the script but many other things as well. The staging is also addressed.

Yes, it is.

"Well, I thought they were going to come from the bedroom instead of the front door, or can we do it from the front door because now it'll work?"

Yes.

You would make your adjustments on those notes. Then dialogue is fine-tuned, "Let's try it with this inflection because we think this line will be funnier if it's delivered in a different way."

Yes, exactly. All those things are feasible and possible. Then the final analysis, the writers make their decisions on whether or not they need to take a rewrite, whether they need to clarify, whether they need to write a better joke, whether they misled an actor, etc., and then I'll get my script on Tuesday night that reflects all of the things they saw in the run-through that they believe that somehow, rather than coming through the window, an actor should come through the front door in a particular scene. They'll write that as a fix for the next revision: "Please have the actors come through the front door."

They have a reason for that. I have no reason to argue with it at that particular point, so I put that into my brain that, when I do that scene, Zendaya will come through the front door as opposed to through the window. Then I realize that it has to be through the window and it can't be through the front door because she has a line about the fact that her hair couldn't fit through the window or something like that. Those are the determinations that get made and get figured out.

When a writing-producing team gets really used to you as a director, and they trust you to stage it, you see them being not so concerned about the stage directions. Matter of fact, you'll notice in most of these scripts they don't even change the stage directions. I will have moved something into the kitchen and they've still got it written in the living room, because they just trust the fact that I can do that. Unless they see something they really need to fix, they tend to leave that stuff alone.

That's what's important about the producers' run-through.
You are basically auditioning your work for the producers and your job is to put on its feet the best performance of their vision that you possibly can so they can look at it and determine what they can fix or need to fix or what they can make better. You certainly don't want them walking away at the end of your run-through thinking, "Nothing works, the whole thing didn't work." Because that's not going to get you much employment.

You know, sometimes you get stuck with a bad script. That's a very important aspect to be brought into this. I used to make a joke about, "Please do not give a first-time director the show with the elephant." You don't want them having to deal with the cow, with the elephant, with the baby gorilla, with a lion running around. Give them something a little bit simpler because those are things that can kill you.

Step 5: Writers' and Producers' Run-Through

Making Animals and Actors Work

There are times where there are animals on the set. There are wranglers or trainers who control them, and who are responsible for bringing them to the set and creating a safe environment. How do you deal with animals as the director?

They always say, "The two things to stay away from in television are animals and kids." My career has been involved primarily with kids, who I think are great because you can always count on them to be kids, and with animals, whom 99 percent of the time turn out great because they behave. If you tell a dog to sit, the dog will sit. He's not going to ask you, "Is it okay if I stand now?" He's just going to sit.

But there are a couple of instances where, as I was learning the craft, shall we say, things occurred that were a little strange. My first episode was a *Laverne & Shirley* episode about a guard dog or something. This dog was supposed to snarl and do all kinds of things to scare the girls. That was all fine and dandy so I talked to the trainer. I said, "You got this? This seems like an easy one." He said, "Sure." We were in the middle of shooting and I found out his way of cueing the dog to snarl was to run on the set wearing a yellow raincoat, blocking three of my cameras from shooting it. I asked, "Is there a way you can cue this dog from behind the cameras?" [*Laughs*] He said, "Well, let me see if he can see me in my yellow raincoat from behind the cameras."

We managed to get that shot, but that wasn't as big a problem as *The New Odd Couple.* Demond Wilson and Ron Glass. By the way, I might mention that the *New Odd Couple* was a big mistake because they decided they were going to redo the original *Odd Couple* scripts, this time instead of using 40-year-old altacocker Jewish men, they were going to use two very good looking, 30-something black men. Different cultures. Okay, that wasn't really the problem. The other big problem was they miscast Ron Glass. Somehow because Ron Glass was very very erudite and sophisticated and kind of metrosexual, they translated that into neurotic. Well, Ron Glass wasn't neurotic. He wasn't even close to neurotic. He didn't have a neurotic bone in his body. It became very hard to pull off that show.

But one day they decided they were going to do the "guard dog" episode.

They were going to bring in this huge Doberman Pinscher as a guard dog that the guys were getting in order to protect their home. Well, nobody bothered to ask Demond Wilson, but the fact was, he had a deathly fear of dogs. The only way I could get that scene shot with the dog was if I played the dog. I was on all fours chasing him around the set so I could get shots of him in panic. I think at that point he might have been scared of me anyway, so I think it kind of worked because here was this idiot director on all fours, chasing him around the set, barking [*laughs*]. That was quite a moment. We learned from that point on, don't bring dogs onto the set when Demond is around.

There's also what we call the great burro episode on *Full House*. Every time this burro came on set for rehearsal, it would have an erection. Now, if you've never seen a burro erection, it is a black hose that's approximately three feet long that stretches all the way down to the floor. I've got the little girls, Ashley and Mary Kate, who are two and a half now, staring at this thing wondering what it is. I've got Bob Saget and Dave Coulier ready to run off 1001 jokes that I'm trying to stifle.

At the point I finally pull the trainer over and said, "Man, what is going on? Every time I bring that burro onto the set, he gets an erection." The trainer says to me, "I think it's you." I said, "What do you mean, you think it's me?" "I think there's something in your scent that's attracting him and that's why he's getting an erection." [*Laughs*]. I said, "Okay, fine, I'm going to walk off the set and let's see what happens." By golly, that burro had no more hard-ons. It was unbelievable. The erection was gone. And, indeed, I had turned on a burro, which was something to be lauded, you know?

Would you advise, then, directors to be careful of wearing cologne when an animal is on the set?

[*Laughs*] All I can tell you is that when animals are on sets, 95 percent of the time they behave better than the actors because they'll do exactly what they're told to do or been trained to do. But every once in a while, boy, you just got to watch out because something strange will happen. Like cows on sets. You can't put cows on anything but carpeting, otherwise if they split those legs, you've lost a cow. There are things you start to learn about the animals we tend to have frequenting our shows.

Step 5: Writers' and Producers' Run-Through

Did you feel the need to do some research when you heard a specific animal was coming to set?

If I knew an animal was coming to set, I needed to know a little bit about what the animal was about. Are they afraid? Don't go up to them. You don't pet these animals. You don't do this to those animals. Usually the trainers will warn everybody if they've got an animal that you're really not supposed to walk over and start to poke around. Like obviously if there's a tiger on the set, you know you're not supposed to go over there and pet it. But you wouldn't know you're not supposed to go pet a cow. You do have to learn tricks with animals, also.

How do you advise a first-time director working with live animals?

That's a very hard question. It's a crapshoot. Animals are tricky and unpredictable. I have a quick anecdote about a tiger on set with Holland Taylor. It's hard enough for the director to deal with the unpredictability but think how the actor feels. In addition to delivering her lines, "nice little kitty, nice little kitty, oh, no need to get up, no need to get up, you don't have to," and then all of a sudden the tiger gets up. It wasn't supposed to. Now, Holland Taylor's on set with a loose tiger. She somehow worked the entire scene and made that scene happen, and we got it on camera. It was unbelievable. She was so scared. Finally there came a break and the wrangler called the tiger off set and the tiger ran out the door and we were able to get back to Holland and shoot an ending for the scene that was appropriate.

Now what about during the producers' run-through when you don't have the actual animal?

I play the animal.

[Laughs] Do you recommend that to other directors?

Only if you're a lunatic [*laughs*]. I played the animal. I just get on the set. I bark if I'm a dog. I move around. If I'm a lion, tie me down. You've got to tie animals down to a spot. You're not leaving them roaming around a set. I remember doing the *Shake It Up* episode where the whole apartment's a wreck and Rocky's sick and Flynn disappears and CeCe comes home and they got these puppies running around the set. I went to them in five seconds and said,

"These puppies aren't running around the set. You can forget about that. You can't contain little puppies running around the set. Put them in a place where I can contain them. Keep them off to the side and they will become a cutaway because it was much too much." You never would've survived that.

Joel Zwick can do that. Can another director do that?
Wow, no, but another director could go over to the producer and say, "Do you want me to actually build a wall in the front so they can't get out? I don't know exactly how you want me to deal with it." I would've dealt with that at the production meeting. I would've said, "Guys, you've written the stage direction here that these little puppies, six puppies, are running all over the place."

Step 6: Applying Producer Notes

Day 3: How to Improve the Play

This step is when the notes given by the producers on Tuesday are applied to Wednesday's rehearsal and changes are incorporated in the pink revised table draft to prepare for the presentation to the network. This rehearsal includes all the bells and whistles: props, special wardrobe, stunts, special effects—everything. Joel also discusses what to do if any element isn't quite ready for rehearsal.

Preparing for the Network Run-Through

It's not a good idea to try something for the first time in a network run-through, and probably not even for the producer's run-through. But the difference is, you can show something that's a mock-up in a producer's run-through, but you want to show the real thing if it's a prop or a wardrobe gag for the network run-through.

Yes. There's no question that the evolution during the course of a week of the production grows. Remember, it's being built around you as you are rehearsing. Perhaps there's a new set that's being built like a hospital operating room. There's a scene that's going to take place in this operating room. Now that's not going to be a finished set, so Tuesday, basically the writers will be asked to use their imagination for certain things that we have not yet accomplished or been able to get props that we were building, special effects things. By Wednesday the job is to add elements besides the writing, which you have all kinds of things being added. Now all of a sudden the prop guy has got the right props and you're putting the props into the scene. But you have to remember the actors are still reading scripts, so sometimes trying to get them to read a script and hold onto a prop can kill the rhythm of the scene. You have to make that judgment on your feet. Forget the prop for right now. We know it has to be there. Use the script as the prop or something. But by Wednesday we want to be more specific. The network wants to know what the robot looks like.

Whatever I can come up with in giving them more production value on the network run-through, we will go for. And that has to do with how complex or simple the specific needs are. If it's a complex need, everybody may have to buy into the fact that they might not see it until God knows when. Also, you will schedule the shoot so that the scenes that have more complex physical needs don't get shot until the second day of shooting. You don't put them on the first shoot morning, you put them some time on Friday so that on Thursday, the producers can look over and talk to hair about the wig that they're supposed to be getting for so-and-so.

Now staying with the network run-through, you don't want to show the network anything for the first time on the day you're shooting.

That's a very good rule of thumb.

If you can't incorporate it into the rehearsal or even the run-through ...

I will show it afterwards.

And do what we call a "show and tell."

Do a "show and tell" on a special effect for example. This is the way the confetti is going to blow out of the envelope. This is the way this is going to happen. The robot's going to move like this, especially if I didn't get the robot until after my work was done in the morning. It probably showed up after lunch. So we will do "show and tell" on those things so that we give them as much information as we have.

If you also have a good enough first AD, he'll understand the importance of sound effects for the network run-through.

Yes, they tend to do that. You tend to be very big on that. I've had varying degrees of that, but you're very good with that. You get the CDs of all the sound

Step 6: Applying Producer Notes

cues, music cues, whatever it is and you try to fit every one of them in there that you possibly can unless I tell you, "Let me just go 'knock, knock' instead. It will be much quicker if I do the sound effect myself." Or you'll pick up a megaphone and decide to do a line because you know that you can do that line better than some other person trying to pretend to be a police officer at the scene of a crime. We basically all play the game of trying to create the greatest illusion of as great a show as possible and that's what we do. We do whatever we can do. But, to get anal about it, it can come back to bite you in the butt. It really can because … it's just not going to happen. If you spend so much time trying to make it happen, you're going to be crazy about the fact that it's not happening. That just takes away the energy from what the cast needs, which is a buoyant day of rehearsal leading them into a buoyant run-through.

If something doesn't work in the network run-through, then the chances are it's going to be cut.

Could very well be, unless like I said, you have powers as a director and you can tell the producers, "No, it didn't execute right. Stick with your writing. I can make this happen." You might get an okay: "Let's leave it alone until we see what goes on there and we'll have alternatives ready just in case."

But also, if the network doesn't get to see a prop or a gag or a special effect or a stunt …

They're going to be worried about it.

As mentioned, we can show them afterwards. And if you get a prop late in the day after rehearsal of that scene has already been done, the rule of thumb is you just don't show it in the network run-through.

You don't. You don't put anything into a network run-through that you haven't been able to rehearse. That's crazy. There was one time that Rob had rewritten a scene, he wanted to see the rewritten scene and I did not get that rewritten scene until just before the network run-through. He said, "I really want to see the new scene." I said, "You know that I haven't even worked with this new scene, but they're all in the same positions, let's just read it and see how it comes out." You can do certain things. There's no hard and fast rule about what that's about. But the producers don't really want to do that. Nobody wants to put themselves in a position where they're showing something to the network the first time it's ever been shown. Then you take your notes and we all get ready to go on to the next day's work, which is the actual day of blocking and shooting.

Run-throughs usually have a specific time that they're scheduled.

Every week when I was doing … I call them the grown-up shows, or even like on *Full House*, we would basically do our run-throughs about four o'clock in the afternoon. That was a standard time. The kids had their school. The kids did everything they were going to do. We had a chance to put the kids into the scenes after lunch. The kids weren't even involved with me. I had stand-ins doing the kids on *Full House*, until after lunch when all the stand-ins gave the blocking to each kid individually and it was unbelievable to watch. It was like this little factory going on there. Each stand-in with their own actor pushing them through a scene, telling them "Just stand here" and "Then on that line, you're going to cross there," "On this line you're sitting on the couch." And then, bingo, now I put the scenes on their feet so we have until four o'clock at least for a three hour run with all the cast there before the run-through. *Shake It Up* ran differently. We did two o'clock run-throughs. A lot of that had to do with the Disney Channel schedule of run-throughs at different times for different shows so that the same people who are in charge from Disney on multiple shows can get to all these run-throughs. It's nice to leave early, but their three hours of school makes it tight for two o'clock … well, sometimes they can finish school after we finish the run-through, which helped.

Then you had dance rehearsals and so many other factors that work into the day. In the old days you would be able to either push a run-through or pull it up, depending.

Here you were locked. But that's okay. Everybody gets a time frame that they're working within a system that is concrete. Every once in a while I'll hear that they're moving the run-through up to 2:30 or even pushing it to 1:30 because of some problem with the network and you just adjust to that. The key is efficiency, vocabulary that creates efficiency and how you as a director view what the job is. What do you think your job is as a director of a

Step 6: Applying Producer Notes

sitcom on TV that's primarily driven by the needs of the writers and the network? And not by the needs of the director. It's truly remarkable. I have no problem with that. Get on a feature thing and all of a sudden I'm in control of everything the way it's supposed to be. Get back to a sitcom, I can't do it.

Give me an example of a director's control.

When we did *Shake It Up*'s "Made in Japan" episodes, our little movie, our ten-day wonder, I went over to Rob and I said, "Rob, this is a feature. This is a feature and I'm going to have to direct it like a feature. I'm going to have to be going back to what I did when I helmed a motion picture. I'm going to have to be in control." He looked at me and he said, "Wow. Okay," and he bought it. I was really proud of him because he'd never done this. He'd always been a TV guy, in control. And all of a sudden a director's coming up and saying that on his project, "I have to be in control or we don't survive. We don't make it happen. We don't get it done. I'll give you as much time as I can give you to do whatever work you think you can get done. After that, boy, I'm the one who decides how we're shooting a set. I'm the one who's making all those decisions, not you. You cannot make those decisions because I have to know I can shoot it like that [referring to time]." And he bought it. But it's a different job. You can't confuse the two jobs.

Step 7 Network Run-Through

Day 3: Performing for the Network

Now you are ready to flex your muscles in a highly energized environment. You get to perform in front of the bosses with an even bigger audience than the day before. You're called on to use your best judgment regarding props, special effects, wardrobe and all the particulars. Afterward the network will give their notes to help shape the final product. This is the last step in the rehearsal process before you get ready to shoot. The network should have a clear understanding of how the script plays out by the end of the network run-through.

Importance of the Network Run-Through

What is the importance of the network run-through?

For me, it's basically to once again push the process, elevate the process so that whatever we accomplished on Tuesday, we're much better on Wednesday. The script that the writers have written is coming to life much more. The problems in it are much less. There are less things they have to address. Maybe a better joke at the end of the scene. Maybe it's too long and they've got to make a trim. They wanted to see it one more time and they realized they've got to thin down the script.

You have a 22-minute show. The most length you want to know about is maybe 25 minutes. If you got a show that's running in rehearsal and run-through at 28 minutes, well, you've got yourself six minutes of length that needs to be trimmed. That's a lot of material. So they need to be able to see this next ver-

Step 7: Network Run-Through

sion of their script. Get a sense of how long it is. Get a sense of where they have to do some better jokes. In some cases, they may have to do a little more rewriting depending upon the nature of the story and how well they've told the story.

Sometimes it's not how well they tell the story. I mean, it is always how well they tell the story, but if they have a good story, we will produce a great episode. If the story they've chosen for whatever reason is a little bit iffy, we're all going to be battling through the course of the week to make it as presentable and exciting as we possibly can, knowing all along that this was not the best story.

This whole thing of network run-throughs changed over the years. In the early days, the network would send one of their coordinators and they'd send somebody from standards and practices to make sure that even in those days we weren't doing anything that we couldn't get away with on TV. They'd send somebody who was basically a creative person out of ABC or CBS or whatever. In those days, if you had a strong producing team, the network had very little they could do about it. They had very little input. If I'm working a Miller-Boyett show for Warner Brothers, let me tell you that if Miller-Boyett and Warner Brothers don't want to do a network note, they just didn't do the network note.

There were stories galore. I wish I could remember his name because there's a wonderful anecdote about Gary David Goldberg, the producer of *Family Ties*, the Michael J. Fox show, really bright guy. They did the reading of the pilot episode and at the end of the reading the network said, "Okay. We have our notes now." If memory serves me well, he said to them, "Excuse me. There are two jobs I can do. I can either produce this show or I can listen to your notes but I can't do both." The network never showed up again. That show was a huge hit and once it's a huge hit, the power went right in the hands of the producers because what is the network going to do, come down and tell you, "I'm sorry we're going to yank *Cheers* off the schedule because you didn't take our notes?" I don't think so! Not going to happen. But nowadays, especially working for the Disney Channel, you have to remember that the Disney Channel is not just the studio, it's the network. It's the co-producer. They are the major voice in the network run-through. And usually what happens, is the network run-throughs run right from the beginning to the end. The only notes during the course of this run-through are taken by the network. At the end of the run-through, the executive producer, line producer, network executives, script supervisor, first A.D., a couple of other department heads and myself all meet in a room someplace to discuss the notes from the network.

The producer will either argue with the note and say, "Okay. Yeah, I understand what you're doing there. Yeah, we'll fix that," or decide "Well, let's try it again," or whatever. Negotiations that go on. But the network representative at the Disney Channel is a very powerful figure. Eventually I sit there and they will give acting notes to me with things that they thought the actors didn't quite get at this particular run-through or things they thought they had better at the table read and lost a little bit since.

I will take note of that and I will think in terms of my own work, is there anything I could do so that the actor can make that moment happen better? I'll do my homework. I'll wait and once again on Wednesday night, emailed to me will be the next version of the script which will have all the changes that the network asked for, that the producers decided will be worth doing. I simply go through it and I take a look at all the changes ...

That version is called the shooting draft.

Step 8: Shooting the Show

Day 4: Preparing for the Shoot

This is the film school portion of the book that is essential in understanding the shooting process. This chapter goes step by step through the technical side of shooting a situation comedy.

The Shooting Draft and the Technical Crew

Now we have the shooting draft that comes out Wednesday night.

Yes, the shooting draft where I take another good hard look at the revisions. At that particular point, one has to determine to do the work of preparing yourself so that when you go in the next morning, you can camera block your staging and shoot these scenes. Whether it's with an audience, without an audience, it's the same thing. Four cameras, go.

Right. They'll be also be cuts in a shooting draft that you may have to restage and incorporate any other changes.

Dialogue changes. The dialogue changes, the dialogue coach is working with actors while they're going through makeup making sure that they're aware of all the changes and that they got their lines down. They're running lines, they're preparing lines. He gives them thoughts about, "Oh, don't miss that word. That word's important to the rhythm of that line." We have a great guy in Tony O'Dell, who had a successful run at acting for six years on a sitcom. He really knows the terrain and he was very useful to us. He will work with the actors in terms of the dialogue and anything that they modified. If it necessitates and takes a modification of staging, I will do that as soon as they come out to the stage.

Before you show the scene, you have to restage the scene. Sometimes you'll ask the crew to walk away so you can have the set alone with the actors.

Whatever I need to do within the time frame that once again the AD has set out for me. I'm starting the scene at 9:30. You expect me to be out of this scene by 10:15. You've got a timeline and I've gotten used to the fact that if you're off by more than five minutes, it's scary. It just doesn't happen. So I'm going to work within that timeline and I'm going to modify the staging. Either stuff that I decide is going to change because I think I finally figured out a better way to do it or stuff that I have to change because the writing has changed. I'll get that done before we start to block the scene with cameras. Then with all of the cameras and boom guys there, we are now ready to break it down.

The thing that you do have to remember, is that these guys know their jobs. The cameramen know their job. The soundmen know their job. They're going through the script. They know which mic is going to be on which person. They know how they're going to move from mic to mic. They're doing all that work. I have no input on that at all. Very rarely do we have a problem where the scene is so complicated that I have to do something for sound to help them out, like if there were wide shots and because of the wide shots the booms can't get in close enough to really get good dialogue because we would see the boom in the shot. I promise them that I'll do a closer pass so that they can get their booms in. We'll do that but that's finessing the problem.

Definition of Framing and Composition

Give us a quick description of the composition of shots that you will assign to the cameramen.

There's the ECU or the extreme close-up, which really means that you're inside the person's face. You're not even seeing the top of their head. Then there's the close-up which probably could cut somewhere a little below the neck. Then there's the Ts, which is basically the shot that crosses the bottom of the chest, be it male or woman and that's a T-shot or medium shot.

Step 8: Shooting the Show

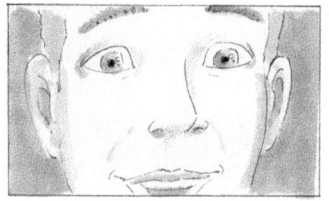  

ECU   **Close Up**   **T-shot or Medium Shot**

Then you have the cowboy shot, which was determined based on the old westerns where the end of the gun hung so that you were getting the gun in the shot. You can cut at the knees, you can cut at the ankles, you can cut full figure [long shot] and insert shots for detail. Those are ways of describing the size of the shot in a sitcom.

Cowboy Shot   **Full Figure or Long Shot**   **Insert Shot**

Nowadays you don't have to worry too much about lens. In the old days you had to worry if you were going to use a 50mm lens at 15 feet, but now with hi-definition [HD] and with video the way it's working now, we don't worry about the actual lens. We've got lenses on our cameras that go from probably up to 100, 150 down to 15 or 10mm. Those cameras, they could shoot a shot across the street and be in focus.

We're not worrying about that but you still have to worry about where you want the shot cut. You want the shot cut at the Ts, you want to cut at the waist, you want to cut at the Cowboy because you know the nature of the action that that person is going to be doing and therefore you know if the shot has to be looser or has to be tighter. There's other vocabulary then. We talked about it earlier on in terms of the permutations and combinations that can be done with four cameras at a given time, how that breaks down. How you use that. We'll deal with that more specifically when we get to camera blocking but that's also vocabulary.

My cameramen need to know what they are shooting and it should be succinct. There are directors who are going to go, "Well, you got a single. Let's do this. Why don't you shoot the single and cut him about here? Well, okay, now you're going to have CeCe and Rocky in a two-shot and you'll keep them kind of loose."

If you're sitting and describing shots to the cameramen who already knows the shots, they're so bored with you at that point. All my cameramen has to know is you're shooting a single, you're shooting a Ts shot, you got the master, you got the cross two. Match them up, boys, and they do it.

They can match them up because they have a device on their camera in the viewfinder ...

That can see what the other cameras are shooting.

It's a quad split of the four cameras so that they can match their frames. This is also on the monitors at Video Village where the director and producers sit and watch the scenes while they are being shot.

That's right. The quad split also allows the cameramen to match their frames or I'm going to tell them I'm not interested in matching frames because the way the set is working.

Now we number our cameras A, B, C and X. Okay, strange numbering. They took a film system and they moved it to tape but I fight with it every week. Anyway, so A, B, C and X. Being behind the cameras looking at the set, the A and the X cameras tend to be the wing cameras and the B and the C cameras tend to be the cameras in the middle. The cameras are spread across the floor.

These cameras pretty well know they're going to be shooting the person who is talking in their direction. They're not going to be shooting the back of somebody's head. These cameramen have been doing this job for many years. They understand that and they see the scene and they know that I have to be looser in this shot. The person just picked up a book, for crying out loud, and I don't have it.

Basically you just have to know what information is really needed to get

Step 8: Shooting the Show

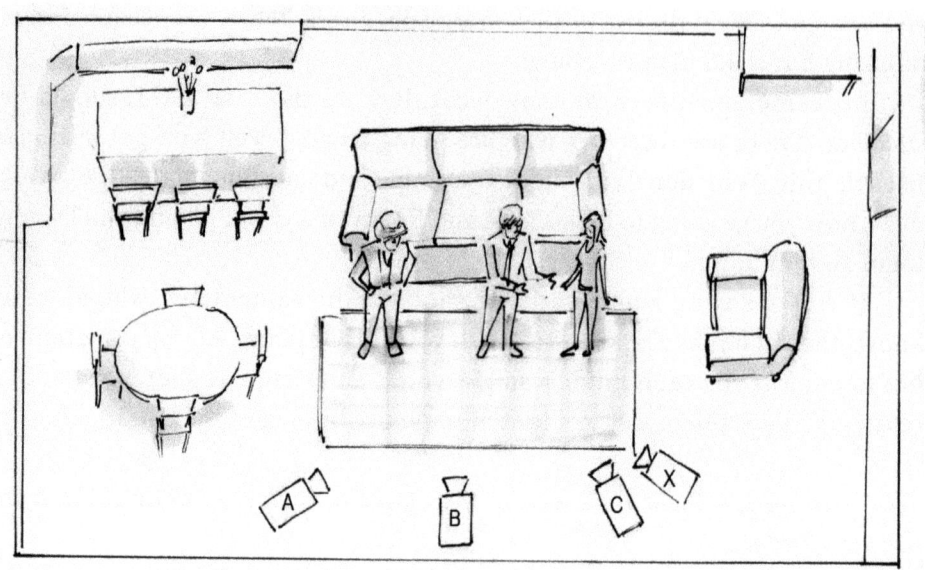

Camera positions

Quad Split

to the next place. If you're giving too much information, you're basically wasting time and it could cause you more difficulty than not. But by being overly specific, you can get yourself in a lot of trouble. So keep it simple and you can get through camera blocking really fast.

While we're on the subject, you positioned the actors while rehearsing way back to the blue revised table draft just for this step.

Yeah, basically like you said, I block the cameras from Day 1. All that work we're doing on the scenes is to get ready to work on Thursday and Friday to start shooting and camera blocking now with the crew, the actors are already staged.

You also explained to the actors the particulars of the scene.

I was teaching them why you can't walk on that line, why it is you can't be leaning forward and back on a chair during the entire scene. I explained to them the discipline that the actor must bring in terms of hitting marks and basically being able to replicate what you do each time so that we match you. Any take I use, you're good in. All those skills that sometimes even an older actor who hasn't done much film needs to learn. I will try to teach those skills. At the beginning, Bella and Zendaya didn't understand a two-shot or a single. It made no difference, but boy, it soon became graphic to them. These girls know that if they're in a two-shot, they are in a two-shot. They are not splitting up, they're not messing around, they're not in no man's land I like to call it where they're halfway between what should be a really good two-shot and turn into a really ugly single. I try to correct those habits and teach them that art because that's an art they're going to need for the rest of their career. Any time they do anything that's visual that necessitates shooting, they will have marks that they will have to hit. They'd have to be able to redo everything they do, repeat themselves so that you have matching that's working out. True, we have our script supervisors, dialogue coaches, ADs, all kinds of people who will notice the mismatch and bring it up and warn the actor, "No, no, no, your legs were crossed when you started that scene."

We've all jumped on that bandwagon but now because we all jumped on it, we very rarely run into problems with the girls. All of a sudden, they seemed to be able to match themselves at the beginning of every scene. We taught

Step 8: Shooting the Show

them something that's going to become critical to their careers after the sitcom.

I directed one of the first couple of *Mork and Mindy*s. Robin Williams was insanely funny. I finally went to him like I did with Bronson Pinchot and I said, "Robin. I've got to tell you something. If you want some of this stuff to wind up in the show, you better hit your mark and stay put. Then do anything you want that comes to your little brain, it's fine, but if you think you can wander around this set without hitting your marks, none of it will make it into the show because the cameras can't adjust to you wandering about." He took that to heart and, boy oh boy, he became really good at that. He knew that he wanted his best work in the show, he had a plan.

Right, but you'd also told them in rehearsal where the cameras are going to be. You either tell them your camera's over there, your camera's over here, and then all of a sudden you see the actors move a little to the left or they'll move a little to the right to help find the camera when we are blocking.

That's according to the script.

They'll also open up to camera.

That's right. They learn opening-up techniques which are very specific to sitcom. You're not going to do that in a feature. The shot is set and you don't have to worry about it but when you're cheating a little bit on angles because the sitcom world cheats on angles because if you shoot over actors simultaneously you'll be shooting each other's cameras. You've got to flatten out the cameras a little bit so that they can shoot the overs from a different angle and now at that angle, there's an opening-up that's necessary by the actors.

You help that process during the rehearsal with the pink revised draft.

Yeah. I think during the third day of rehearsal. The Wednesday rehearsal, the pink revised draft, I try to clean up all that stuff. So when these characters face the cameras starting on Thursday, they know exactly what they're doing and I already know exactly how I intend to shoot it. Now, I might have to make modifications because once again now, we will have a network run-through on Wednesday.

Definition of Framing and Composition

Can you re-iterate the key to shooting?

Once again, I think you have to begin to develop for yourself the most efficient use of vocabulary to say what it is you're trying to say, so that everybody you're talking to could understand rapidly and efficiently what it is you're asking for. We have the certain expressions that have existed in the business forever which we described earlier. The ECU, the close-up, the Ts, the mid-waist, the waist, the Cowboy, the knees, the ankles, the full figure. The cameraman will look at the shot you're asking for and this is where the communication opens up. He will say, "You want me to have a single of so-and-so but so-and-so is using her arms quite dramatically." He knows his shot has to be loose enough to be able to incorporate those arms. That is not the appropriate time for a super-tight shot of that particular person, and 95 out of 100 times, these cameramen will get you the most visually satisfying shot that you can expect. They do that for a living. You do not want to micromanage what cameramen do because they start to go into this mindset which is, "He's going to tell us exactly what he wants, fine. Then I will give him exactly what he wants, but I will give him nothing else. I will give him no found shots. I will not suggest to this person that perhaps while I'm doing that, I might also be able to get this for you. I will not do anything but give this clown exactly what he's asking for." If you're that much of a control freak, that you're going to ask for everything you want and get everything you want, you're going to basically cut off the independence and the input of some very talented craftsmen who've been working those cameras for years and years and years.

You may have to make adjustments in order to get the eyes right or capture a position you might not be able to normally get.

You hopefully have staged it so that these cameramen are doing what they tend to do. They will always have "good eyes." If you stage in places where it's virtually impossible for the camera to get in and shoot so that you can't get "good eyes," you've created a problem. We'll talk about this in detail later. You've got to stage where the cameras can shoot, or if you want to stage into corners of a set where the cameras are going to have a very difficult time accessing that, you have to be sure that there's enough time in the production schedule to basically accomplish the shooting, which will take five times longer than standard shooting. You just have to balance that out in the course of shooting an episode, of where you can take the time to do some very interesting shooting and where you just simply have to churn it out, because you don't have the time to reinvent an entire sitcom every week when you shoot it. You have to have enough stuff that's essentially rote.

Actors know the set. They know how to live in their sets. They know where to stand in those sets to get the best shots based on your blocking. You have to leave yourself time for a little bit of creative camerawork, or a little bit of inventiveness that you think the particular story you're telling might warrant that, but that has to be figured out. You can't arbitrarily just do that. You have to know you have the time for it.

Camera Shots and Coverage

Now we have an understanding of staging the actors for cameras and the importance of having a vocabulary to communicate to the crew. We are into Day 4 of the weekly schedule or Day 1 of shooting.

Day 1, two shoot days, right. To rehash, we talked about that I got the shooting draft Wednesday night after the network run-through. I reviewed the script and I did my homework in terms of any changes I have to make based on the script changes. Then I have to finish up conceptualizing how each scene is going to be shot. However, by that time, I've already done most of that homework. Up to Wednesday, I've been placing the actors exactly where I need them so that there are not going to be any questions. I know how the revised scene has to be shot. I will basically go through it in my brain, mark some things down on a piece of paper if I feel it's a particularly complex scene. I think any beginning director has got to write in a script exactly what the camera blocking is. How you do that and then how you're capable of communicating that to cameramen is really critical. As discussed, that's where you lose time; and time is of the essence. You need to find a system that describes the shots in your script, such as a two against the one, I'm going to do cross threes on this line. I'm going to do a two against one in a single of so-and-so on that line, I'm going to do cross twos on cameras B and C on this line and I'm going to do the singles on camera A and X.

Camera Shots and Coverage

But that's all in your script at this point. Now it has to be seen through the lens of a camera. Sure you can focus on one actor when he's speaking and you can say that's either a one-shot or two-shot. That's the easy stuff because that's either the A or the X "flanking" cameras. The tricky part is telling the story within the two flanking cameras, which are the ...

The two middle cameras. The B and the C cameras.

So how do you approach telling the story with those two cameras because obviously the flanking cameras A and X adjust to what B and C cameras are shooting in the middle, which are traditionally the wider shots.

Yes, obviously the outside cameras tend to be the coverage pattern. Here you have a two-shot on the A camera against a single on the X camera.

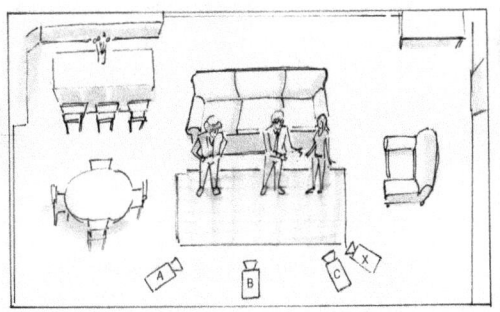

Camera positions

Two Shot

Single

Those are my crossing cameras. Now, I may decide that I need the B camera to be the master in this particular scene.

Step 8: Shooting the Show

How do you come to that decision?

Because I need the C camera to be a matching two-shot with the A camera that is shooting a two-shot from his angle. So now I've got these two people covered when they turn to talk to each other. I know this because I staged it for this purpose. Should it be the other way around, should the A camera have the one-shot and the X camera have the two-shot, I then would make the C camera the master so that the B camera can be a cross two to match what the X camera is shooting. That's just the math of the situation. That's the way you would deploy four cameras with three people in 90 percent of the cases. Now, if I have three actors stationary doing dialogue, this is how I would cover the actors.

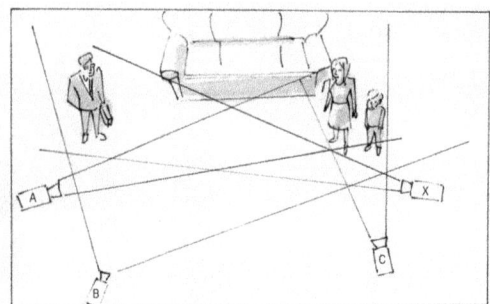

Basic coverage of 3 actors   **Quad split of 3 actor coverage**

But every time somebody moves, it's a redeployment of the coverage pattern. So, let's say, I have my B camera, which is the master, and now the woman starts to move and the B camera's carrying her and she stops someplace else. At this point, maybe the configuration will change.

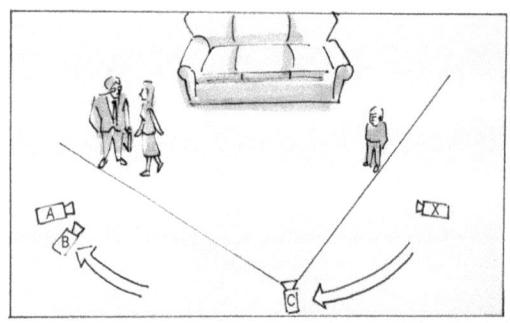

Coverage of an actors cross   **Quad Split after an actors cross**

Now, there's a two on one side and one on the other and at some point I have to get that resolved so that's where it gets a little tricky as you keep moving through the scene because now you will need to have the C camera as the master. So, again the B camera's the master carrying them over to their new mark. Now, that same B camera has to become the new over while the C camera switches to the master. You just have to make sure that you're not caught without any master. You have to carry the people over to where they are going in the master and then once they're there, you now tighten up with the B camera to get the coverage and you open up the C camera which becomes your new master.

But that's all you can do and that's the system. The system just keeps going like that until you decide that you want three singles as opposed to a two-shot against a single.

So the basic formula is that you shoot wide and then you move in for coverage. And with four cameras ...

You have most of your coverage done at the same time unless it's really a strange situation where four cameras leave out somebody who needs to be covered, in which case that's your list of pick-ups, which are done after you've completed and are happy with the performances on all the cameras that are being shot. You have to choose something to leave out for pick-ups; obviously that's not as critical. The key core of the scene you have to catch hot. You cannot be planning on the key core of the scene in pick-ups. You have to assume that whoever you have situated for a pick-up hopefully is an addendum to the scene.

Reactions?

I don't have to shoot reactions hot. I'll give that up hot in order to be able to make sure I have the story covered with the inside coverage and the master that's necessary.

How do you decide where to place the cameras?

I've already placed the actors in the set, so therefore these cameramen already know where they're placed. They already know where they have to be because they've also shot these sets.

Step 8: Shooting the Show

Well, it's easy to say that for the A and the X cameras, but what about the B and C cameras?

Like I said, I'll go over to them and I'll let one of them know that he's not the master in this situation: "I need you for the cross two-shot. Please match yourself off with the A Camera. I'm using B camera as the master." There are areas where this stuff gets more complicated. Permutations and combinations of two people we understand. It's four cameras covering two people. Either they're going to be singles or they're going to be in cross twos and that's it. You don't have much choice. If they move places, maybe they move from being together to apart, so when they move, they become singles. When they come together, they become cross twos. Add a third person and you only have four options. You can either make that a two-shot against a single or make it the other way, single against a two-shot. You can make it where there is a two-shot and cross two, a single and the other a master. You can also have three singles on three cameras and a master on the fourth camera, depending upon which gives you the best coverage of eyes.

I did that at a table. I had three people sitting at a table. I decided that I'll put Ty [Roshon Fegan] on camera X sitting in a chair. I'll put Deuce [Adam Irigoyen] on camera A sitting in a chair and smack in the middle of them was Tinka [Caroline Sunshine]. I put her on camera B. Everyone had their own single. In this case I had over-the-shoulder singles on cameras A and X. Then I took camera C, which I knew I could use as the master because I was going to get Tinka up and cross her to the bar and that would have kept her in the master.

Camera positions for Table scene

Quad split of table scene coverage

Camera Shots and Coverage

It would be a much prettier shot than if I switched it around and gave the C camera to Tinka and used the B camera as a master because it's just the angle that they have to arrive at.

The angle that you see is the optimum angle for these shots and you're right, it's easy for A and X to see exactly what it is they're shooting. You have to define for cameras B and C what it is they're supposed to be shooting because they both think of themselves as master cameras and most cases, one of them isn't the master. You just have to determine who the master is and who's doing inside coverage.

However, they both could be masters. One could be the main master, the other one could be a cross master.

And you have those choices too. It depends. If there are two people, you certainly have options. You can use crosses on the side cameras. You can use one camera in the middle as a flat 50–50 two-shot; we call it "square up the middle." And then the third camera can be possibly a wider master, more of the room entailing maybe including the TV that they're looking at. There comes another scenario if they're both sitting on the couch looking at the TV, you'll have the single coverage on the couch, you'll have a flat two-shot and you'll have the master with the TV in the foreground depending on how you and your cameramen like to see those shots.

Camera positions for two people on a couch

Quad split of two actors coverage

That's a framing choice. I work with the cameramen the same way I work with the actors. I want the cameramen giving me their best eye. I'm not inter-

Step 8: Shooting the Show

ested in telling them what I think the shot should look like. I'm going to tell them the parameters. You have to have the TV in the shot. Then they're going to go ahead and they're going to frame a shot for me that will use their acumen, the fact that they've trained for years doing this job to give me the best-looking shot with the TV in the foreground that they possibly can. Maybe I'd have to do a little negotiating if they missed a little bit of what I want, but I'll reinforce the fact that I want them to be free to find these shots themselves, just like I want the actors to be free to find moments themselves. I can sit above it all and I know that the choice the actor made didn't work or that the cameraman needs to get slightly tighter or give me slightly better eyes. That expression "better eyes" in a sitcom comes up a lot because the cameras are basically flattened out as we discussed. You have to get the cameras further into the set to get better eyes like I did with A and X with the two people sitting on a couch. If I didn't move the cameras into the set, then every time each actor turned to the other actor, we would lose one of their eyes in the shot.

Bad eyes would be ...

One eye. You want two eyes and you want the most two eyes you can possibly get without the cameramen shooting each other. Comedy is not a genre that plays well in profiles.

The Proscenium and Its Multiples

The proscenium is the basic understanding of the way that the multi-camera system was set up to work. We talk about how you need coverage here, you can shoot a one-shot against the two-shot, you can shoot cross threes, you can do all of that. However, what we never really discussed is that multi-camera sets are proscenium sets just like in the theater. They have three walls, or some combination of three walls, and a big opening in the front which in the theater would be a proscenium. For us, it's the fourth wall. The cameras operate within that proscenium opening. However, the proscenium of the movie you're going to make is not the same as the proscenium of the space or the opening that might be in the theater. The proscenium that you create is shot by the master camera. The master camera, I don't care which

The Proscenium and Its Multiples

camera it is you designate as the master, it could be any one of the four cameras, but that will be the one that gives us our proscenium through which the audience views the scene. Then we have the option to go inside of that, to do inside work within that proscenium. To give ourselves the singles and the two-shots and the three-shots, and whatever it is that we need to tell our story. What the proscenium gives us is not only a general picture of the world that we're looking at, but it gives us an orientation of how the singles and the two-shots need to be shot. Because it teaches us the looks. We will understand then that a character in the proscenium is going to be looking camera left to camera right, or a character in the proscenium is going to be looking camera right to camera left. We have to then shoot our inside coverage with the correct look so that the character in the master that's looking left to right also is looking left to right in your inside coverage.

This works 99 percent of the time. It may not work quite so well if you're doing a card game or a family dinner where people are sitting around a table, where sometimes the looks are not dependent upon what we see in the master, but might be dependent upon how people talk to each other at a table. That's a little more complicated than I think we need to get into, but this whole idea of the master camera being the proscenium now teaches you the fact that we will have multiple prosceniums in the course of any shoot. As long as everybody is in the same position, you've got one proscenium, now once the proscenium changes because the master camera is taking a different point of view towards what the scene is about, that takes us to a different part of the set, shall we say.

Which an actor can carry you to.

Right. Now all of a sudden, that new proscenium has to be addressed and in that new proscenium we have to determine whether the looks are left to right, right to left in the master. We also have to set up the prosceniums so that we can, when shooting our inside coverage, get the best eyes possible on these shots as we discussed. To reiterate, "best eyes" means we want the look of the actor talking as close to the lens as possible, so that we're seeing what we call "two eyes" as opposed to an eye and a half, or in some instances only one eye.

Step 8: Shooting the Show

The Importance of Resets

If it's a lengthy scene and there's a lot of movement creating multiple prosceniums, you are going to have camera resets or rolling resets. Tell us why there are resets.

You've got four cameras deployed in the kitchen area of *Shake It Up*. There's a scene that got played there, now CeCe is going to cross from that particular spot into the living room and sit down on the couch and Rocky is going to follow her.

Which is on the other side of the set.

Yes, so there's no way those four cameras are going to truck along and make that happen. So what I will do is a reset. I will have them start out in the kitchen and shoot the part of the scene in there, then as they leave the kitchen to enter into the living room, I'll call out "reset" and I'll move all the cameras into the living room, send the actors back into the kitchen before they enter the living room and pick them up as they re-enter the living room, creating a new proscenium, and continue with the scene.

Matter of fact, the story was that in the beginning [of TV], when using film, it was always a three-camera situation. Always three cameras from the

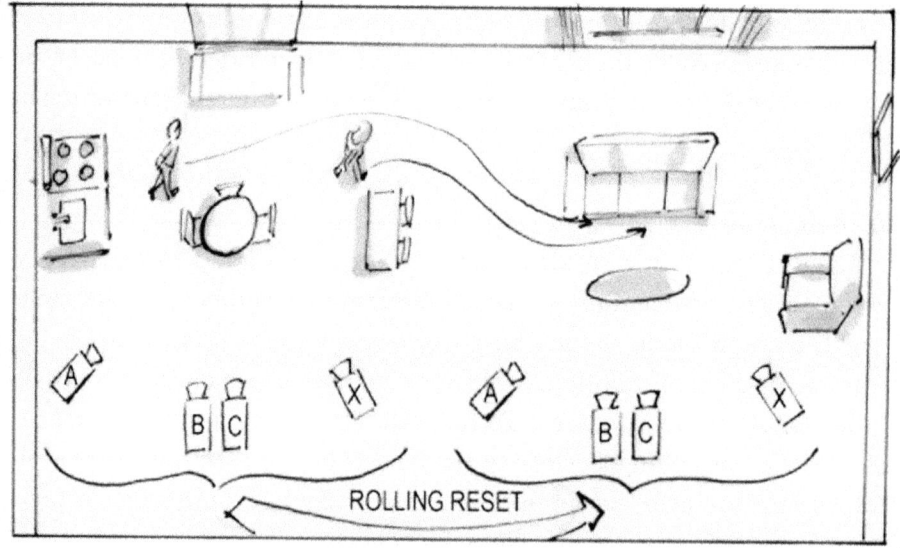

Diagram of a rolling reset

time that Desi Arnaz came up with how the hell to shoot *I Love Lucy*. Three cameras so he could get the audience reaction live.

Jimmy Burrows had a problem when he took over *Taxi*. The garage was so enormous, he couldn't get the job done with three cameras. He begged the producers to give him a fourth camera, thus the X camera came into being. It was Jimmy and *Taxi* that set that little thing up. That was still shot with film at the time and basically he needed that fourth camera so that if he was going to move somebody across the set, he had a camera waiting who can handle a bit of the cross while the other cameras kind of caught up and got into the action. In addition, *Taxi* had many lead actors and they needed the additional camera for coverage.

Those were cameras that had dolly grips, and dolly grips can move the cameras so the camera operator was only worried about framing the shot with the assistant cameraman responsible for focusing. When you're dealing with peds and HD cameras, which is the way we shoot sitcoms today, basically the camera operator does it all. He has to move the camera, he has to keep his eye on the shot and worry about the focus at the same time. That was a three-man job in film, it's a one-man job now. Therefore, the idea of video cameras being able to fly over great expanses of space yet holding onto the shot, I wouldn't put too much stock in that. There were guys who were pretty good at it but you wouldn't want to live with that, that was just craziness.

You just talked about rolling resets. That's easy enough. You described how Jim Burrows had the X camera designated to carry the action over while the other cameras were resetting while still rolling. Then you'd go back and overlap the action once your cameras were reset. A lot of times if a scene is too long, you would have several resets. You were so ingenious on knowing exactly when you needed a reset. Unfortunately, this is where a theater director is going to have difficulties ...

Big time.

... because now the flow of the scene is going to be disrupted. Talk a little more about that. Why it's a necessity to have multiple resets and how that director will have to adjust. The best way to do it is to go from one reset, get it clean, then move on to the next.

Step 8: Shooting the Show

Yeah. We finally made that determination on *Shake It Up*, but part of the problem with *Shake It Up* was, I had a scene going on that's maybe a page and a half and then all of a sudden Zendaya comes in through the window. Okay? Clean coming through the window. I make the determination; I can't have Zendaya sitting out there on a fire escape waiting for me to get through the first page and a half. I'm much better off cleaning up the one and a half pages and then I know I have a clean entrance on Zendaya and continue to the next beat. Then I also know that I have a clean entrance on Davis Cleveland [who played Flynn] coming out of his bedroom later and I can bring that action in after Zendaya's reset is clean.

All my resets are based on two things. Garry Marshall taught me, you always get a clean entrance on everybody coming in and you get a clean exit on everybody going out. Basically you can do wonderful things because now matching is not so big a problem. I'd say about 90 percent of the time that they would tend to fall on either the B or C camera, but it might be by the nature of the set or the nature of other things that are going on. It may actually be the A camera which will very often give me an entrance or exit into or out of the apartment stage left. To further clarify, stage left is the actor's left side facing camera. Stage right is the actor's right side of the set as they are facing the camera. So camera right and stage left are the same but just called something different depending on who you are addressing.

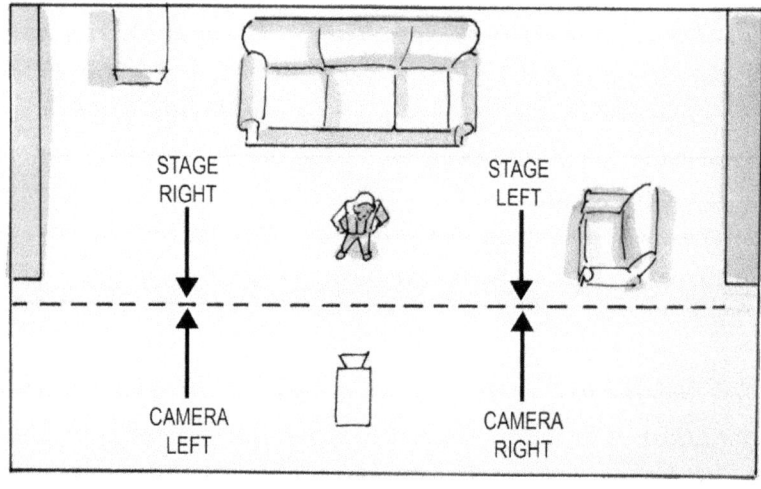

Camera/Actor set perception

The Importance of Resets

You'd also have varying sizes of entrances and exits?

Yeah, I have the ability to do it all. I'll shoot one loose entrance and then I'll shoot it slightly tighter. Of course, because at that point I'm deploying my cameras, I'm getting set for this entrance. I've got four cameras now, I will get the angles I need to be getting. Let's say there is a girl sitting on a couch and another sitting stage right at a desk. I will shoot my coverage of these actors before I reset for an entrance.

Camera placement to cover an entrance

Quad split coverage before the entrance

Now the actress is coming in through the front door, and I've decided to take a reset before the entrance. I've got the A camera and the B camera bringing the actress in from the camera right door.

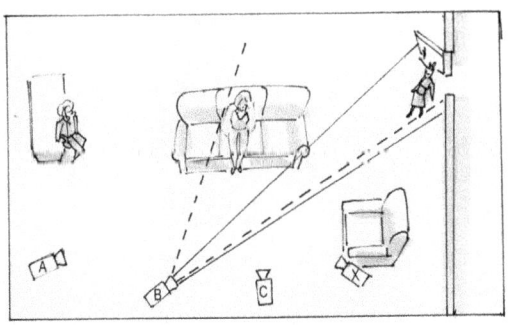

"B" camera coverage of the entrance

Quad split inc. "B" camera framing movement of the entrance

One is pretty loose, usually the B camera, and the one bringing her in tighter will be the A camera. She will then cross to the couch from right to left where

Step 8: Shooting the Show

the X camera will be coverage on the two other girls. The A camera will still be on the actress who entered, the B camera will be looser and widen out to a two-shot to bring her over and the C camera will be the master shot of all three girls.

Another example?

Let's say there are two girls sitting on a couch and I have my coverage before a reset for the same entrance. I have matching two-shots on A and X, a flat two-shot on B camera and a master on C camera.

Camera positions for 2 actors before entrance **Quad split coverage of the actors before entrance**

Now the same actress is coming in through the front door, and I've taken a reset before the entrance.

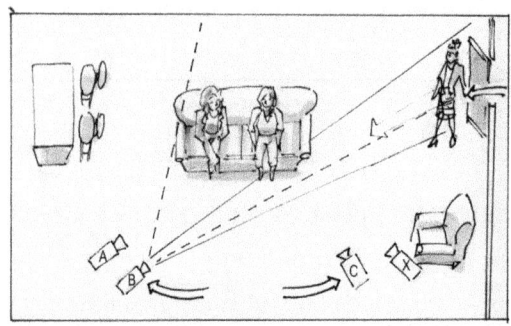 

"B" Camera movement to cover the entrance **Quad split including the "B" camera move's framing**

Now, I've got the A and B camera bringing the actress in from the camera right door. One is pretty loose, usually the B camera, and the one bringing her in tighter will be the A camera. She will then cross to the couch from right to left where the X camera will be on the two other girls in a two-shot. The A camera will still be on the actress that entered, the B camera will then widen out to be the master to bring her over and the C camera will be the cross two shot of the girls.

There also seems to be more control in a long scene when using resets.

Absolutely. And you know something? Producers love it, too. They can control a part of a scene, see the scene and say great, that's terrific. Can I do that one more time? Let them do it one more time. Let them do it two times and then you move on to the reset and you go back maybe a line, pick it up and go again and now it gives the producers a sense of control as opposed to if they had to see, let's say, an eight-page scene in one fell swoop, then their ability to give notes and to understand what they need shot-wise becomes broken down. It's a lot to keep in their head. It's a lot to comprehend. So, if you can break a scene down to three little "scenelets," let's call them, there are three different prosceniums that can take a reset in this scene that let them control one reset section, let them control the second reset section and then give them the third reset and you'll usually find yourself moving much faster through the scene than trying to do the entire thing.

The Short Wall

Talk about this concept that you call the short wall.

This has to do with the changing prosceniums, when you create a proscenium that's, let's say, against a wall. Lockers in a hallway, lockers in a schoolroom, plenty of shows have lockers in a hallway. And every time people are at a locker in a hallway, you're on what's called a short wall which means that the actors are against a wall. Now you can shoot any angle of master you want, that's not really the problem. You have some range of master. What you don't have any range of is how you get these people standing by the locker to get the best eyes, especially if you don't, because usually if it's a short wall, you don't have a return.

Step 8: Shooting the Show

You're not able to shoot this way, this way and this way. You probably have to shoot that way, that way and that way. Which means you have to stage appropriately for the short wall, which means your proscenium is no longer flat against that short wall, but it's angled at 45 degrees so that you can have some person at the locker, some person kind of standing in the hallway talking to them. If you put them both against the lockers talking, the chances are you have one angle and you don't have the other angle because there's no fourth wall or return wall there. You basically run out of wall, making it a short wall.

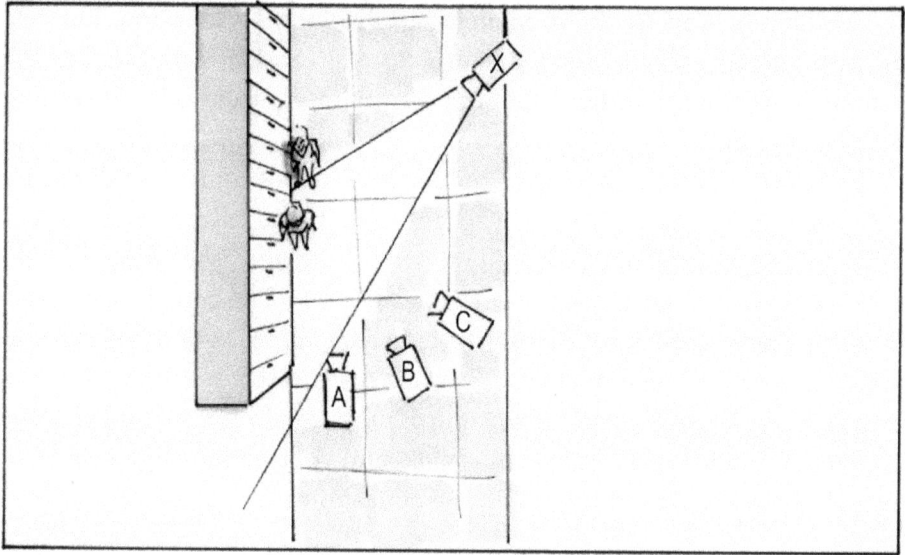

Shooting off a short wall set

So you only have one angle on one actor. And then you don't have it on the other actor.

You have to modify how you set up your master. I call it the short wall theory and it can be on either side, it doesn't make a difference to me where you have to reposition the actors and usually I set my masters in those instances at something of a 45 degree angle, so that they are not against the wall together. Plus, it's not as pretty a master.

So you always pull them away from the lockers.

Always away, that's right.

Pass Coverage

Blocking adjustment for a short wall

The other thing that you have to now be aware of is 16:9 as opposed to 4:3.

You know it, because the 16:9 creates a bigger problem when you do have short walls because you're possibly going to shoot off the wall. So you have to really position things and to be quite honest nowadays even though a Disney critical is 4:3, 16:9 is industry standard and everybody clears and makes sure that they have critical information in 4:3 but they're definitely not seeing anything they're not supposed to see in 16:9 like shooting off a set. And that's the rule of thumb.

Pass Coverage

Now let's talk about multiple pass coverage.

The concept of multiple pass coverage is once again mathematical. You'll have just four options of what you shoot with four cameras in any single pass. The minimum you're going to do each scene is twice, to give the actors a chance to warm up into the scene perhaps, but that would be in just one pass coverage layout. During that pass coverage you must make sure that you clean up every-

Step 8: Shooting the Show

thing you need from those four angles of coverage including better eyes. In the second pass, you might modify camera positions for different coverages. You might be able to get in the second pass a pick-up of somebody you haven't shot yet. Let's say there are five people in the scene and two people are sitting together, constituting a two-shot. One person is standing by herself, that's a single. Another person is sitting stage left by himself, that's another single. The fifth person is sitting stage right by himself. Now I've got the master shot that will include all five people, but I have not gotten any close-up or single on that one addition or fifth person sitting camera right—stage left.

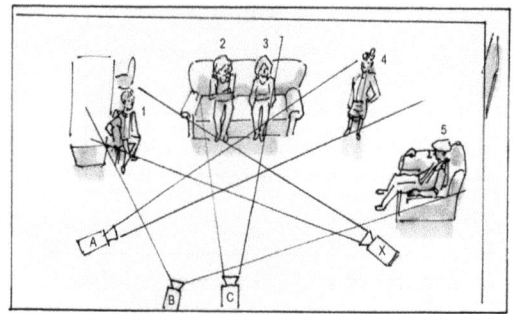

**Camera placement for 5 actors;
1st pass coverage**

**Quad split of 1st pass
coverage of 5 actors**

I have to then plan that as a pick-up on a second pass using one of the cameras that we're shooting one of the other singles to shoot that instead, that's what I would do. It's still a mathematical equation. It's just organizing who gets left out of the shot if you have too many people to cover with four cameras in any given pass.

You also have the differentiation of the framing where you might be a little wider in the first pass but in the second pass, you'll cover the same four people in a tighter shot and that fifth person is still left out until a third pass.

I may choose to do that for different sizes or I may be able to get that fifth person in acceptable second pass coverage by switching just one of my cameras to cover that actor as I previously said in one size. That's maybe all I may need if the producers are okay with it. Otherwise I will need the other size as seen in the diagram.

Conceptualizing the Story with Four Cameras

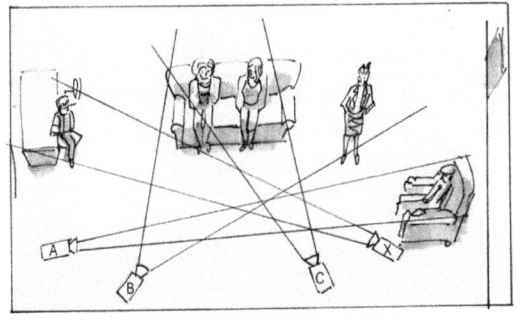

Camera placement for 5 actors; 2nd pass coverage

Quad split of 2nd pass coverage of 5 actors

Those are the judgments that you make as you're moving through any shoot of any scene. Producers also have their input on line delivery; they don't think that such-and-such did the best line-reading at such-and-such a moment. Can I get that again? Yes, you can, of course. Therefore, maybe the fact that I was going to switch coverage for the next pass, I couldn't do it this time because I still had to get a performance that the producers or the network wanted. That's just the internal moment-to-moment work that has to get done as you're trying to get the best performance and the best shots in camera so that the editor can get together and put together a bang-up show.

Because of everything being shot in HD today, you have the capability of enlarging any shot up to 25 percent of its size without any loss in visual quality. Which means, if you're going to err on any side of framing you're going to err on the side of framing a little looser, because you always can tighten it up in post. You can't open it up in post. You cannot make something wider if you shot it tighter, but you can make something tighter if you shoot it slightly loose. If you're going to make a judgment error on how to shoot a shot, shoot it a little loose and in post when you're looking at the shot you go, "Wow. That shot should really be a little tighter." It tightens up in no time at all.

Conceptualizing the Story with Four Cameras

How do you conceptualize and subliminally help tell the story with four cameras from beginning to end?

I have to understand the relationship of the actors in a scene, and stage

Step 8: Shooting the Show

the actors in the scene, as I believe their relationship warrants. If it's a situation where two people are arguing with each other, I will determine whether they should be very close to each other arguing, or they need some distance arguing. The physical truth of it—it's really a basic of physical mathematical truth—is, if the people are close enough together, you're in two-shots. If they are far enough apart, you're in singles.

For me a master is containing all the people who are critical to the scene, who speak, who help tell the story. A super master might include more people than just the talkers. It might involve a crowd that surrounds them because that is what the story needs for the audience to see. It might even involve a much wider shot than that. Usually, that's why I call it a super master that involves maybe two people sitting on a couch, watching TV. The super master might be the shot that includes the TV, whereas the other shots are basically coverage. When you break down the scene, you'll have to understand what must be covered; what the coverage must be to tell the story. Now, two people fighting could be done in two shots or could be done in singles. You'd have to determine how that works out for storytelling. Do they have to be close to each other or should they be far apart?

Now, I'm telling the story with cameras. If let's say there are three people, and two of the people are arguing with one person. Well, that's probably a situation where you're going to put the two people in a shot against the one person they are arguing with in a shot. That will tell the story that they are separate entities, fighting each other, or arguing with each other, or discussing with each other, but there's definitely two people against one. Three people could also be three people each in their own individual shot to tell that story. That's the director's determination of how he best tells that story, but mathematically, that's all you got.

Now, you may have to go in and do some pick-ups. The powers-that-be may say to you when you're doing three shots, "Wow. Is there something we can do so that I have some ability to cut into that three-shot?" Well, with four cameras, I could do that, too. I can take my A and my X camera and do cross threes, so that all three characters are in the shot. I can use either the C camera or the B camera to be a flatter three-shot from the front or the master. I can use the other camera to be a single of somebody in that three-shot that might be able to help in terms of defining the moment.

Conceptualizing the Story with Four Cameras

Camera placement for 3 actors **Quad split of Single coverage preference**

You would choose the shot based on who the most important person is in the three-shot, who you'd put into the one single. That's usually the person in the middle of the three-shot who tends to be the most important person in the shot that somehow seems to be the reason why everybody's clinging to them. That's a question of how you see the story, but that's how you manipulate cameras to tell the story. What is the argument of the scene? Who needs to be in the two-shot and who needs to be in the single? That depends upon every script individually, but in the final analysis the solution as to how you cover the scene is mathematical.

But you also start with a wide master shot as a rule of thumb, because you're never going to start a scene for the most part on a single.

Correct. Usually, I have to do some kind of establishing shot at the beginning of scenes, so that we understand where we are, and the relationship of all the actors to each other. Now, whether or not you need the super master to start the scene is once again a directorial choice. Let's say they're in a school hallway and you need to show the energy of the hallway. Well, then you would start with the super master, but at some point, you don't want to go the super wide shot every time you want to go to the master. You'd like to have a tighter master that includes the speaking people in a full figure shot. It's in that tighter two-shot master, in this case being the C camera, that you have a couple of options. You can do what we call "the carry." If there are two people talking, and the woman leaves and crosses to talk to somebody else, in this case you do a "carry" on the C camera while I also carry the two-shot over to the lockers on my B camera which is my current master.

Step 8: Shooting the Show

Camera placement for a super master

Quad split of camera assignments with a super master

Now, I've got her talking to somebody else by the lockers in a two-shot which my full figured master [B camera] will maintain [a full-figured version of C2] while the C camera carries the actress over maintaining a tighter two-shot [frames C1 to C2]. Ninety-nine percent of the time, all mastering gets done in the middle, by the B and C camera.

Commercial Breaks

Commercial breaks are determined pretty much by the writers. They have determined that a sitcom currently is written structurally. Maybe there might be an opening teaser and then a first act. Then you go into your title sequence, which is pre-shot with credits and a theme song, because it exists for every episode. Then you go into Act One. At the beginning of Act One, you'll have to establish where you are visually, and you'll have to do the same when you go out at the end of Act One because you know it's going to be a commercial break, with some kind of a picture that's meaningful. It could be a little girl crying. That might be the close-up shot that you want to go out on, if you believe that's the important thing in the story. I mean, *Full House* ended virtually every act on a close-up of baby Michelle. It was a joke, as a matter of fact. It seemed like no matter what was going on in the episode, they wanted to end on a picture of Michelle who was crying, or hurt, or sad, or happy.

You don't have to go out wide in a master shot. You can go out in a two-shot if there's an emotional or funny climax to a scene that gives you your act out, you have to just give them the shot that sells that. Like I said, it could be a close-up, it could be the two-shot, it could be two girls fighting, it can be somebody stomping out the door, and the other person looking at the door like, "Oh my God. I just lost my best friend." Then you need to sell that in the shot and that's what you go out on. When you come back in from commercial, rarely would you come in tight. You could go out tight. Considerably, often, you may go out tight. Usually, it's very hard to come in tight. You got to get the viewing audience reoriented to where they are and to what they need to see.

So you probably would come in on a master shot of some kind that reminds us where we are, what the relationship of the actors are, if that same poor person is still staring at the door [*laughs*] because she was hurt at the end of the first act, I might come in with a wider shot. If I could include the door in that shot to see what she was looking at, I might do that. I would have to determine based on the needs, but I certainly wouldn't come back in on a close-up of the same moment that I just left even though the script may say "Act Two—continuous."

Step 8: Shooting the Show

Whenever there is a lot of physical action at any point in a scene, you can guarantee that you're going to probably cut to a wide shot.

Yes. You can't play physical action in close-ups, that's for sure. And that's just something that's obvious. You just can't do it that way. You have to stay with telling the story. If the story is a physical story with two people rolling around on the floor, grappling with each other and somebody is tickling the other person, you're going to have to be loose enough to see what going on.

Traditional Camera Blocking with Stand-Ins

Let's touch upon the traditional way of blocking and shooting because your way is somewhat rare. For most directors coming in, the protocol would be that they come in with their idea of how to shoot a show with four cameras in their marked script and it gets presented to the camera coordinator. Then the camera coordinator will help fine-tune the shots, and those notes will get conveyed to the cameramen and then the director would perform the camera blocking segment of the day. Sometimes you have the morning dedicated to camera blocking and rehearsing with stand-ins and sometimes you camera block and then immediately shoot the scene with the regular cast. Tell me in more detail about the camera blocking portions of the shoot day.

For 99 percent of the situations, we have stand-ins who are hired that give us enough bodies to portray each of the main actors in a given scene. Each of these stand-ins do their homework and write their blocking down in their scripts during rehearsal days. They write everything down that they're supposed to do, so that theoretically, when it comes time for camera blocking, the director and the camera coordinator can block with what we call second team or the stand-ins. While the first team [the principal actors] are either in makeup or finishing school or doing a dance rehearsal or God knows what else they need to do, you will be using stand-ins who basically do two things for you. They move from spot to spot as they do the lines so the sound department gets a chance to see and hear the scene, and secondly the camera department gets a chance to see what the shots are that you're asking them to shoot.

There are different ways to do that. When I used to work with stand-ins, I did not get myself overly involved with them performing for cameras. Other directors may feel differently. But with regards to my approach, I simply move the stand-ins myself. I didn't care whether they had lines to say or not. I would say, "Stay put. Okay, do we got the shot?" I would point to the cameramen and say, you got the two-shot, you got the single, you got the master, good. Now I would move the stand-ins to their next position. Now (pointing to cameras), you have a single, you have a single, you have a two-shot, you got the master, great. Then I would move them over to their next position and I'd literally walk them from spot to spot giving the cameramen their shots for the entire scene. I was not trusting whether the stand-ins remembered the spots or whether the spots they hit were going to be the exact spots. I moved them where I wanted after I knew the cameras saw what they needed to see because watching them perform is not the same thing as the first team. The rhythms are different, the blocking is different, the body language is different. You might decide with the stand-in that it's okay to shoot Ts across the chest and then the first team comes out and you find out that you got to shoot her with elbows because you're missing her hands. It just changes. To waste your time as a director trying to direct stand-ins to do this work is insanity and any experienced director who directs stand-ins is really missing the point when they spend too much time blocking the scenes this way.

However, for the directors that are starting out, there is value in using the stand-ins because it does help develop their process.

True.

Specialty Shots: Do You or Don't You Reinvent the Show?

When you have a camera on an actor who might be sitting in a chair and another actor entering the room behind him, sometimes you will just slide the camera to pan up to the person entering or you pan up to the actor in the chair. How do you come to the decision of doing those kinds of moving shots within the one camera?

That's stylistic. You just have to be very judicious that in those carries you've already gotten the gut of the scene taken care of. You can't do your fancy carry

Step 8: Shooting the Show

shots and say, "Oh, I'll carry this person to this person who will then dump me off on this person who will then carry me to the door and they're out" unless you know that each step of the way you have all the coverage. They don't want the carry shot in post. If they have to cut out some information in your carry shot, they have the option to do that too. These gloriously inventive camera moves ... which sitcom isn't the world for, but if you want some of them, make sure you have the scene and the coverage completely done. If everybody's happy with all the performances and then if you have a little time and you have a fancy shot that you want to pull off, go for it. That would be the safest way to do that, especially if that's not ordinary vocabulary of that particular show that you're on. If the show that you've watched episodes of and they're carrying people all over the place, then yes, you have to pick up on that style. But the more you deviate from the style that it's currently being shot in, the more trouble you could get into. Once again, the best thing a director can do to impress people with their acumen is to do the show the way the show's always been done, not to reinvent the show. No matter how brilliant you are, don't reinvent the show. They're not going to be happy. They don't want to reinvent the show.

A first-time director should get episodes to watch?

Oh yes, any show. When I do any show that I've never done before, I call up the producers or somebody and ask, "Please send me three episodes that you consider to be the most representative of episodes that you've done this season." I get them and I study them. Then I go down and I view a camera blocking day. I view a shoot. I can see the sets now, I see how they're shooting the sets. I can see this. I can see that. From watching three episodes I can start to put together how that show is shot. If I see things that surprise me and I go, "Why in the hell did they do that?" ... that's where my system starts to come to play and when I get in there to do my work, I will not try to change how the show is shot, I will try to change how the efficiency of the show is shot.

Give me an example of how you would do something more efficiently.

Dog with a Blog. I went in to do one episode of *Dog with a Blog* and asked for three episodes, studied the three episodes. It's a funny show. It's a funny concept. A talking dog is a funny concept. It worked with Francis the Talking Mule. It's working for a talking dog. It's some funny stuff. I thought the cast was very good. I got a sense of what they did. The adults on that show were very sharp and very efficient and very crafty. The kids are pretty damn good.

I go in and I'm watching it being shot and all of a sudden I'm realizing they're stopping the scene to do the pick-up of the dog exactly at the point in the scene that the dog is supposed to do something. And I said, "Wait a second, that's crazy." You have to have all four cameras getting me all the dialogue. Now, if the dog is in a master, yes, the dog comes to a mark and sits. Fine, the dog is in a master. I'm not going to pick up that dog until that scene is in the can. Then after the scene is shot, I'm going in and will start to shoot the dog. I have four cameras to shoot that dog as the dog is doing stunts or I can put a person into the shot with the dog; take a person out of the shot; I just have to plan it so that I have all the things, all the information I need from the dog. It takes a little more planning, a little different planning, but to stop every time the dog is supposed to do something and to set up the shot for the dog is not an efficient way to shoot. The momentum of the scene is now dead. That was what I spotted with that particular show. Then you define other things that you get a sense of how the stage works and you come down to the camera blocking. Do you have a strong AD? Do you have a weak AD? How's the camera coordinator? Does he have a lot of input? He doesn't seem to be saying anything. I love the onstage set dresser, I did *Pair of Kings* with him. Funny guy, he works his head off, terrific. I wasn't sure about the dialogue coach. I didn't understand her. I didn't quite know what she was doing. I need to find out more about her. What was going on with her? Why was she giving notes at a time when she shouldn't be giving notes? Why weren't her notes going through the director? That kind of stuff. What was going on? What was the politics of that situation?

Once again, trying to learn the politics, so that when I got there, I was understanding how the situation was working and I could make adjustments, making my time on a show more efficient.

Is Shooting Comedy Formulaic?

How did you train yourself?

Well, for me, the bottom line is why you call me a one percenter. Why is it that I can visualize these things? Why is it that my mind seems to be fast enough to be able to handle all this disparate input from hundreds of people who have problems that they're trying to get solved and I simply can stay with it? Well, I trained myself to do that. When I did my first *Busting Loose*, I memorized my camera blocking. I didn't look at the script even then. I memorized it. I knew, "Okay, you're going to be a two-shot, you're going to be in a single...." I literally would do it that way. I had it all memorized shot by shot by shot for the entire scene. And that's why three scenes in, I went to Phil Perez and said, "I've got nothing." Like I said, Phil helped me get through it. But I knew at that particular point that that was a challenge I thought was a critical thing to accomplish if you wanted to direct sitcom. That you didn't work with a script; that you listened to the actors; that you were their first audience; that you laughed when you found things funny; that you didn't laugh when you found things not funny; that you were responsive to them. You were there with them, not looking at a script, you're there with them watching what they're doing.

During rehearsals, I have a script supervisor or dialogue coach who will tell the cast if they said words wrong. I'm one to find out if the humanity of the scene, if the flow is working, if the crosses are happening, if the places I put them are the right places. I have to watch that. I can't be looking at the script. I decided up front that I'm simply never going to use a script and I forced myself to memorize my camera blocking. What you see now has evolved to this almost instantaneous stage that doesn't even exist.

Which is not going to be helpful for a first time director *[laughs]*.
No, it's not going to be helpful, but the skill that is helpful is the amount of hard work that I put in and it wasn't because of anything other than just a hard work ethic. Lower middle class Brooklyn, you understand, education was critical; hard work is critical. If you did those two things, you have a shot at getting out of the lower middle class and maybe getting an apartment with a terrace that I never did get that I wanted so desperately. And those are the goals. I was just a hard worker.

The fact that I thought of things to work hard at that worked out well for me, may be smarts, may be luck, may be any number of things, but somehow I knew that I wanted to be with the actors. I didn't want to be with the script. I knew that I wanted to be able to learn how to visualize what this movie was all about that I was making. I didn't want to worry looking at a script to determine it. I wanted to see it in my mind's eye and I started to train that.

Yes, 600 episodes, by golly I can see shots quicker than the shots show up. In the beginning, it was hard. I spent a lot of time poring over these things, writing out specific notes and then memorizing those notes and trying to find a way to simplify the notes so I can communicate to the cameramen or to the actors more efficiently what it was I was looking for. I built that into my system.

Is there a formula for how you compose your shots from the beginning to the end of the scene?

Well, only if the scene or the storytelling demands it. If the storytelling is going soft all of a sudden, it might warrant a tighter shooting than if it's free-flowing and kind of loosey-goosey, which will necessitate wider shots so that you can see bodies, especially with kids. Kids act with their bodies. They're not acting with their heads. They're not head actors. They have their whole bodies going. Half the time your problem is getting to control the bodies, so the bodies aren't all over the place, but their bodies are part of their acting. You have to be wide enough with kids to be able to see what their body language is all about. But you're right. If it comes to a meaningful little scene at the end that's about a tear in somebody's eye, I hope you're shooting tight enough to see the tear. If not, then don't even do the scene. There's just certain things we all understand.

Which brings me to the quote by Buster Keaton, "Tragedy is a close-up. Comedy a long shot."

Yes, essentially Buster Keaton lived that. It's a general enough statement, but you have to stay loose enough with comedy because comedy's about body language just as much as it is about facial stuff. As a matter of fact, the facial stuff may look a little bit too large for a real close-up because sometimes a situation comedy tends to play slightly broader than one that's not played for laughs.

Right, because you want to keep the audience at a distance in order to bring out the humor.

Well, yes, it's objective. The cameras are doing objective work. The camera is not another character in a sitcom. The camera is basically the audience's

Step 8: Shooting the Show

point of view. It's the master that's the most pure audience point of view and the cameras that are shooting inside coverage are shooting POVs of each other. They're inside, but you have always something that's representing the audience point of view in a sitcom because that's who you're playing it for.

And wide shots obviously work better for comedy because it's funny to see both the comic and the straight man at the same time.

That's not even just a wide shot. That's why you make a two-shot of basically Tom Hanks and Peter Scolari or Laverne and Shirley or Ethel and Lucy because you wanted to see them together working the situation out because they knew how to play each other. When you get into those things, when those people know how to play each other, you can put them in a two-shot and let them play with each other rather than forcing yourself to cut singles for everything that they're doing. Comedy plays much better in two-shots than in singles. No question about it, unless there's a real fast repartee and you think you have to pop singles [snaps] to get that argument going. You're much better off in two-shots.

You've talked about editing while you shoot. You're looking at the four cameras. How does one prepare to shoot the quad while knowing that the frames will be cut together?

That's just about the toughest question you could have possibly come up with. A lot of it has to do with experience. What I did initially was, I basically trained before I ever shot my first show in the editing room. I went to the editors, I went to the camera coordinator. I wanted to find out and they would say to me, "See that? That doesn't cut, but do you see this? This cuts. Do you see that? That crossed the line," etc. I just thought, "To log this information, I would have to live in that editing room." At that time it was Bob Kern, who's a wonderful old editor who was doing *Laverne & Shirley*. He would just take me through it, "This is why this can cut." I would start to get the simplest version of why things cut together. If somebody is looking left to right at somebody, the other person has got to be looking right to left to be able to see that they're looking at each other. You start to find where the lines are and where you can cross the line and how things can fit. Your vision gets more complex as you get better and better at that. Luckily in sitcoms, since four cameras are shooting simultaneously, virtually everything that's being shot will cut, it will, it has to. Unless you've done something very strange which nobody will let you do. The cameramen will not point the cameras at each other. They will point the cameras at the person that they know that they're supposed to be pointing the cameras at. If you just leave them alone, they'll do 98 percent of the show without you having to say boo.

When doing sitcoms, virtually all cameras will cut because they're all being shot simultaneously. The cameramen themselves will tell you, "It doesn't cut." I worked with Larry Blumenthal, one of my favorite camera operators. He looked at the quad split in his camera and I asked, "Larry, why are you shooting a master there?" He said, "Well, because the other guys are doing this." I said, "Oh, okay. The other guy is wrong. I want you to shoot the three-shot and him to shoot the master." They'll give you feedback as to why two-shots are too similar to cut together. The cameramen know these things.

Step 9: Adjusting the Shoot

Day 4: Accommodating the Network and Producers

In addition to shooting the show according to your planning, ability and craft, you must also make adjustments if there are any requests by the network or producers. With the help of the camera coordinator, you will need to think on your feet and decide how to best get the requested shot. Joel will explain in this chapter how he works to keep the network and producers happy.

Network Notes and the Changing Industry

You apply all network and producing notes during the shoot and make camera adjustments to satisfy these notes.

Yes. For instance, the network or producers may want to shoot something over again. But I'm going to start it from the beginning of the scene for the most part because usually I like to start from the beginning if the scene is short enough. Starting in the middle just drives you nuts. Therefore, if all they really want is a close-up of so-and-so doing a line, that gives me three free cameras that now I can play different games with than I did in any of the coverage patterns I shot because all they're interested in is getting that line from that person. I will put together a different package of camera coverages that open up another possibility that wouldn't have been possible if they didn't ask me to do that one line over again.

Also in the tradition of the sitcom, where it's the producer's medium, as much as you may feel comfortable and satisfied with the scene, you can't move on until they approve.

Only unless you're creating a time frame where you, as the first AD, are saying, "Guys, we've got to move on. We're ten minutes behind. I gave you extra time." Therefore, the producers have learned that they had better pay attention. So that at the end of the day, if they're missing two scenes because every scene they told the AD, "I don't care about your timeline. We're not happy with this scene." You just lost your kid actors because they had to wrap at 3:30. I hope you're happy with the fact that you missed two scenes.

Even from scene to scene, once the producer said okay and signed off, then the network would have to sign off.

They tend to work together. They both say, "We got it, moving on." On occasion, I say, "Wait a second. I got one more thing I want to do," and it's always a big surprise to them. It's usually by the time they're finished with their hocking and flocking, I've gotten everything I want done because I've been manipulating cameras with Tommy Thompson the entire time off of the original patterns, creating different angles and whatever.

That's it. They're the ones who finally say, "We can move on. We got everything we want." Unless, like you said, you have a real push, which we only had one time on *Shake It Up* where you said, "Guys, you're talking about five things you want. I smell only three things you're going to get. Tell us what it is you can't live without so you can get going with this thing." So then you let me prioritize how we can shoot them most efficiently. Luckily I have experience so that I can survive that kind of insanity.

What can you say about maintaining work based on your style?

Usually track records do mean things. They mean things both positively and negatively. There are producers in this town who wouldn't touch me with a ten-foot pole. I've just got too much attitude. They can't direct through me. They're going to get too much input. They're going to hear things they don't want to hear. They're going to have control issues that they don't want to deal with. I'm too much baggage for them. I met with the guy who created *The Cosby Show*. We sat down. We had a lovely meeting. We looked at each other and said, "There's no way we can work together. We'll kill each other in five minutes." We never did work together. Yet I ran into him a month ago and we still have very fond, warm thoughts about each other, but it just was never going to happen for us.

I tend to work on shows where producers like to have a strong hand, a

Step 9: Adjusting the Shoot

directorial strong hand that's moving their product along. If they don't want that, they don't tend to hire me. You have to have a chemistry with the writing producers and you have to have the chemistry with the cast. They don't know you from hell or high water. Maybe they know of your reputation. Maybe they checked out your IMDb and they went, "Oh, my God. This guy's got to be a hundred."

Also, you have to trust going into an established show that these people know what they're doing.

They do the show every week. All I'm going to do is get in there, have a good time, try to give the writers the best run-through I can, to give the actors the most I can in terms of support for what they're trying to do. Hopefully, if it's a good enough story, we'll turn out a great episode. Always will.

The process will create a great episode, but it's all in the writing. It sometimes takes people who come in as directors and then wind up in sitcom, still thinking that the answer to cinema is a directorial vision, and even in features nowadays, that's starting to shrink. There are very few directors who end up with their vision for a film.

You mean the director's cut?

No—the vision of how this movie should be shot. What do you do with this? What do you do with that? The control you have. Right now, the bottom line in features is corporate. They're not interested in giving you $150 million so you can do what you want. The most amazing thing to me was when the Weinstein Brothers were battling Martin Scorsese over the cut of *Gangs of New York.* They wanted 20 minutes taken out of that and forced him into it. I'm thinking, "My God, if Marty Scorsese can't make a movie the way he sees it, the industry is changing."

There's very few now that can get away with that kind of stuff. You're always on budget. You're getting 40 days to shoot this movie. Not interested in giving you 48, not going to happen. You're certainly not coming back a year from now because you didn't like the way the sun set. Those things are just not happening any longer in the world and the young director believes, somehow, that their job is to know everything, to determine everything, to tell everybody what to do, and that's exactly not their job. Their job is to listen, to learn, to apply their craft, to be political, to be social, and to be smart about what you do and to understand the nature of the job you're being told to do, and try to do it as efficiently, as fun, and as well as you possibly can. If you do all that, if the writing has been great, you might actually produce a wonderful piece of art out of a sitcom.

Tom Hanks said to me recently, "I still think that some of the work I did on *Bosom Buddies* is the best work I've ever done." I went, "Wow." Certainly, he did some great work on *Bosom Buddies*, but the fact was he also did a few other things that might be considered really special.

ature *Like Oscar-worthy things?*

It all goes back to hard work, developing your craft and what goals you set for yourself in terms of the level of craft you want to achieve. How high you set your goals and challenge yourself to meet those goals and challenge yourself to visualize. I don't know how directors work who can't visualize what's going on. I don't know how they work if they're looking at a script, in the hopes that the script is going to give them an answer as to how they should see a scene or shoot a scene or feel the scene or stage a scene or encourage a scene or laugh at a scene. I don't know how that happens. I know that maybe directors do that and have been quite successful with it, but the thing about my style was to basically be there for the actors, no script, memorize everything, and then I began to see all the stuff I was memorizing.

Memorize everything in terms of...?

In terms of the staging, in terms of the flow of it. In terms of the way I'm going to shoot it. Now, I just have to take a look at a scene, I can tell you how it has to be shot. I don't have to memorize it any longer. I'm sure in 90 percent of my staging, you can see how it should be shot. You may not be able to spin it out as fast as I can right now, but I bet you that if you had 50 episodes behind you, you'd be able to spin it out as fast as me if you chose to do that. If you thought that was a useful tool for you because that was getting you more employment and helping you grow in the industry.

Like I said, ten percent of the shots, or even less in a sitcom, have to be designed, you have to really think, "What the hell do I want to do here?" This is a little different. You have to figure this out, like you were concerned about

Step 9: Adjusting the Shoot

why I sat Flynn on that upstage chair so that Leo Howard from *Kickin' It*, who was guest starring on *Shake it Up*, could get stuff out of a cabinet up in the set, then showing it to Flynn, then having to talk downstage to CeCe, who was on the couch. Before I even staged that, I would say, "Okay, how do we shoot that?" I knew I was going to have certain problems, but I knew all the pieces I had to get to make that happen and even the order I have to shoot them in to make it the most efficient to get that coverage.

I've decided I'm going to bite the bullet and stage it that way. I reset for Rocky coming in through the window. Whatever they were doing after that, once Rocky came in the window, you couldn't quite tell if they were exactly matching or not. They'd be close enough for rock and roll.

Step 10: Final Shoot

Day 5: Performing for a Live Audience

This step takes us through a final shoot day. We concentrate on the remaining scenes in the script before the audience show. Joel will discuss the mechanics and importance of this final day and how he readies himself for the audience and how the director's job will be completed in a production sense. There is more to do in post-production, which brings the director's cut to an assembly presentation. Joel takes us through to the point of delivering the director's vision to the next level.

Show Time

A lot of sitcoms are still doing live audience shows. What is the importance of an live audience?

The importance of an audience show, that got started by Lucille Ball, was a chance to give comedic actors a chance to perform in front of a live audience. However, you had to make many more considerations for the quality of shooting in order to accomplish shows in front of an audience than when you're actually just blocking and shooting where you have a little more time to get better angles, to get more coverage, to get all that kind of stuff that you don't have time to get in front of an audience.

Basically, *I Love Lucy* had three cameras and when you try and catch everything in front of the audience, your visualization has to be simpler. It's only three cameras shooting. It's a master and inside coverage.

We have four cameras now.

Now we have four, but the fact is when I started out, there were only three and it was simpler.

Step 10: Final Shoot

What's the advantage of the live audience?

The advantage is the timing of jokes. You get a laugh that creates a sense of timing. Their energy goes up. However, their energy may become a little more cartoony, because they're performing bigger for an audience than when they are for a camera, and the sensibility today tends to not want to do that in most sitcoms. They want them to be a little bit more "real," so to speak. They're not interested in being as over-the-top. Less performance ... more real.

What you gain with a live audience is the laugh spread that it gives you. It makes it harder to do all the coverage you need. It makes it harder to get pick-ups. It makes it harder doing a number of things. That's the reason why the hybrid form came along, in which you try to make sure that you got everything in the can before your audience show. The alternate used to be to do two audience shows, one at 3:00 and one at 7:00. That way we had two passes at it, and between the two passes and maybe one or two pick-ups, you could put together your show. It helped the actors get their energy up, focus up, wanting to perform well. There's no question that was a big value.

If you do have an audience show now, you're not necessarily shooting the whole episode any more.

If there are big major scenes that were virtually impossible to do in front of an audience, you would have them shot the day before or the morning of, put them in the can and actually have the editor cut together some quick version of the scene you already shot and show it to the audience in the proper sequential order. They get to see a whole episode and maybe only see 50 percent of the show being shot live. What turned out to be on *Shake It Up* was that the inordinate amount of time necessary to shoot the dance sequences put us at a disadvantage because doing an audience show lost us about three hours of shooting time a week. Disney decided they wanted the dances to be more visually exciting, therefore, more shots, they had a look, all that kind of stuff. They had to get rid of the audience because we're never showing the dance in front of the audience anyway and it took too much coverage. The average dance was five, six passes and that's if it was going well.

Show Time

The other thing with the audience show is that because you are shooting it in sequential order, you are faced with certain challenges.

That's right, so all of a sudden, you have costume changes and possible hair and makeup changes, and God knows what else you may have to accomplish during the course of the show with the audience sitting there. We were doing a *Full House* episode and we had as a guest star (and I was thrilled about this), Kareem Abdul-Jabbar who for many reasons, many reasons, I was huge fan of. Never mind the fact that he played on the Los Angeles Lakers; it was the fact that he was a jazz aficionado, the fact that he was so outspoken and verbal about the African-American community and all those things. He was a hero of mine and he also came from Queens. I was Brooklyn but essentially he's a New Yorker. Anyway, we're doing a scene and all the scene asked for was for Kareem to hit a sky-hook from three feet away from the basket.

That's his famous shot.

He scored 28 million points in the NBA with his sky-hook. Well, he missed it four times in a row from three feet out, while I'm rolling. I have footage somewhere of Kareem Abdul-Jabbar missing his sky-hook four times in a row.

Was he missing the shots because he was nervous? Did you help him through that eventually? I mean, how did you approach him?

John Stamos ran out. John Stamos who doesn't have an athletic bone in his body ran out and showed him how to do it and eventually he hit it ... [he] showed Kareem how to do it [Laughs].

Showed Kareem Abdul-Jabbar to hit his trademark shot.

That's right, but that's funny.

But that helped him relax.

You bet. John defused the situation for me. He just went in and did it. He just found it to be a hysterical moment and he wanted to be part of the moment. He just got into the moment and showed him how to do the sky-hook and on with the scene.

Step 10: Final Shoot

As a director you were smart enough to know that being a short Jewish man, you wouldn't be able to help the situation. You were smart enough to let somebody take the task [laughs].

Yes, somebody else took over. But Kareem was interesting because we had an announcement to make. He was being introduced as the guest coach for a basketball game that was being played. He was teaching John Stamos where his spot was. If he just gets to that spot, he can always sink the ball from that spot but he has to get to that spot.

Anyway, the opening announcement came and our guest coach is Kareem Abdul-Jabbar, five MVPs, scoring champion, blah, blah, blah. We did this twice and finally I went over to Kareem. I said, "Kareem, excuse me if I'm wrong but I think you have six MVPs." He said, "I do." I said, "Then why are you letting them say that you only have five?" He didn't speak up. He needed to be protected from himself. He would have just bought the five and never said a word about it if I didn't have the knowledge of the fact that he won six.

You did your research on your player.

Yeah, on Kareem, yeah.

Any other special athlete moments?

I'm doing *Hangin' with Mr. Cooper,* a show about Mark Curry who had been a basketball player, six foot five, so he certainly had the length for that. We went up to San Francisco to shoot an episode where he was going to get a tryout with, I think at that time it was the Golden State Warriors, who had Gary Payton and Tim Hardaway on their team. Somewhere along the way, I don't know how it happened, but both Tim Hardaway and Gary Payton managed to "pants me" during the scene. They just decided they were going to rip off my pants and make me run around in my underwear because they just thought that would be funnier than hell.

I've had things like I was doing a rehearsal of *Family Matters* and they're in the stands, waiting till I was finished with the scene, was Michael Jordan and his two kids. They desperately wanted to meet Urkel and father Michael Jordan had no alternative but to sit up there in the stands with his kids so they can come down and meet Urkel. I met Julius Erving, I met … God, it goes on and on, the number of athletes that we used, John Thompson and Patrick

Ewing when he came on to do an episode of *Webster*. The unique thing about that was Emmanuel Lewis, who was about two and a half feet tall, was able to dribble a ball through Patrick Ewing's legs without Patrick Ewing having to do anything. It was quite a sight to see this. That was a fun shot to get.

We did an episode with Dwyane Wade on Austin & Ally. Quite frankly, you never know what you're getting with an athlete. But athletes who are willing to step on a sound stage usually can do it because ...

Usually can do it. They don't embarrass themselves.

They have this feeling that they're comics, they're frustrated comedians and they can make the guys laugh on the court or on the playing field or whatever sport they're in, and it gives them an opportunity to act it out in a different forum, as long as you make them feel comfortable ...

Again it goes back to the old adage, "If somebody comes in that's an elephant, let them be the best elephant they can be. Don't decide that it would be nifty if they became a giraffe." And certainly, if it's an athlete, don't play that game. You got to find out what this athlete can do best and just let them do it and find out what they do and you may get some stuff that the writers weren't expecting because the writers really don't know him. They're just kind of servicing a need, somebody said, "Please, put so-and-so into your show." That's what happened on *Webster*. Patrick Ewing had just signed with the Knicks out of Georgetown and the Knicks were owned by Madison Square Garden or something that also owned ABC. therefore, they wanted to make sure that their new recruit got on one of their shows, so we had Patrick Ewing on *Webster*.

There will be a number of other things that will occur in the course of a career. Good and bad, just last season we were doing an episode of *Shake It Up* and who shows up on the set? Kobe and Vanessa Bryant and their two daughters. Why? Because their two daughters were in love with the girls on *Shake It Up* and Kobe sat there with his wife. We gave them a special place and stayed for most of that show so that his kids could have their moment with my girls. That's something where the kids rule the universe, and the most highly touted fathers in the world are sitting there in the stands with their

Step 10: Final Shoot

kids so that they can meet these people. [While doing an episode of *Jessie*,] I look up in the stands and there sitting in the front row, with his daughter and wife, is Tyson Chandler. Tyson Chandler is seven feet, two inches tall and played center for the New York Knicks. I can't begin to tell you what it looked like when you look up in the stands and you have all these kids with their parents and then there's seven-foot-two Tyson Chandler and we could not convince him to come down to a VIP section because his kid wanted the whole experience of watching from the stands. That was a hoot.

So this is why you pick and choose the scenes that will make the audience show run most efficiently and effectively, which also dictates what you pre-shoot.

Very much so, but that's another scheduling situation for the ADs. I'll have a couple of quick suggestions of things I really want to accomplish. For the most part, you tell me that it's got to be in this order, and I'll go, "Sure, you win."

After you pre-shot during the day, then you have your crew meal. Afterwards, the actors go in for touch-ups and then you do a speed read-through because you want to refresh all the actors. What's the advantage of doing that?

The speed-through helps pick up pace. It gets everybody not thinking, but seeing if they just can spit it out. Spit it out because all you're trying to do is make sure that they remember the words, that they remember the scene. You're not looking for them to act the scene, you're just looking for them to speed through it, which gives pace. When they take that speed-through onto the set, their pace tends to pick up. Which, as you said, is so critical to comedy. If you're not picking up those cues, we're dying. "A truck could pass through that pause" was a phrase we used to say during a shoot if an actor didn't pick up on their cues.

Which you don't want in front of the audience.

No. If you're going to go in front of an audience, you want to get them to give their best performances. You want them snapping and sparkling and hitting it all and doing the best they can. It's trickier with the young kids than it is with seasoned professionals, in terms of not getting too high, too excited, too this, too that. The teenagers will do things that the grown-ups won't do in front of an audience. They just get so hyped up that we can't get them calmed down. The audience gets them going and that's not the show you want to put on the air, either.

To be quite honest, as far as a laugh track goes, right now, they've got laugh tracks that sound better than any audience you could ever bring in there. It's no longer the problem of, "Can you get a good laugh track?" The difference is whether you have people out there already laughing for you or whether you're sweetening everything in post.

The world of sitcoms has come full circle because that was part of the process. You finished off the week with that audience show. It was part theater, part television. You put the play up in front of an audience and you're putting up a production. It was a show.

You were doing a little show, absolutely right. With a curtain call at the end of it, with introductions at the beginning of it, with a warm-up person doing jokes before and during the show. Bob Saget was our warm-up man on *Bosom Buddies*. That's what he was doing to make a living. There were people who made a great living doing warm-up for sitcoms in those days. You needed that. You needed the audience heated up. Somebody to remind the audience, "Now remember the last scene, so-and-so did this and so-and-so did that." All of a sudden we're getting into the new scene. I used to hate when the warm-up used to say, "Remember to laugh in the same place you did the last time we did the scene." I'd go, "No, don't say that," because you get these false laughs, desperately trying to fill the laugh they did the first time. Bottom line, tell a story and get the best performances you can, and let your crew do their job and you're going to come out a winner every time you do it.

The Booth vs. the Floor

What was it like, directing from the booth as opposed to nowadays where you're predominantly directing on the floor?

Let me revisit what I was saying earlier about the history of recorded multi-camera comedy that goes back to Desi Arnaz and Lucille Ball in the 1950s.

Step 10: Final Shoot

Desi got the idea that he wanted to try to shoot the little plays they were doing using three cameras. That's when the system of using multi-cameras to capture a bit of a comedic thing and be able to show it to America came into play. Then in the '70s it became more complicated. We started to use tape instead of film. Tape cameras are much cheaper to produce, much cheaper to post, much cheaper to do anything with, and they decide that now that it's cheaper, we'll go with four cameras, too. That's how the overall concept of using four cameras to capture situation comedy became more popular.

At that point, the way the process worked was that the director who staged it during the week, which remained very much the same process, changed when it came to shooting. The director's responsibility at that time would come from primarily working from the booth. What I mean by "from the booth" is that, he was no longer on the floor with the actors, he was in a room watching the quad split and a fifth monitor that showed a line cut. It was no longer a question of coverage. It was a question of setting up the show that you were directing, shot by shot by shot creating this line cut we discussed earlier which has all the coverage marked in your script. Let's say the first shot in a scene is on camera three [C], it's going to be a two-shot. The second shot is going to be on camera A. It's going to be a cross two shot.

Basically, then the job of the director was to give his shot list or marked script to his associate director. Then he was the one who transmitted the information shot by shot to the camera operators via a camera meeting instead of me when doing so on the stage floor. It would take them about an hour to do this in the morning and they would just sit around and go through the script shot by shot, still not having seen any of the staging. Then, the process continues. I'm in the booth with the Associate Director with others nearby. We have a dry run with stand-ins. I'm still not cutting it during this dry run, I'm still making sure the coverage is what it's supposed to be. Basically, it's working out my timing as to when to cut between shot one and shot two, shot three and shot four. I'm trying to edit on my feet in the booth.

It was probably more stressful than it is now.

Well, yeah. You had to be on the money; you had to be ready to go. You were snapping those shots off. I was one of the more sane directors where you might get a *Bosom Buddies* with 147 shots. But Asaad Kelada was the king. He could come in at 420 shots. We never knew how the hell he managed to stick so many shots into a half-hour. I was getting it done in 190 shots and he was cut, cut, cut, cut, cut, cut, cut, cut …

With a little cricket clicker.

I had a clicker. I had it gold-plated, I've saved my clickers. They're all gold-plated. Jay Sandrich taught me the clicker deal. I was working with my fingers and Jay said, "That's crazy. Here." He gave me a clicker and said, "Try this instead." It was a little cricket clicker. Well, this makes sense.

Who makes fun of me? Jimmy Burrows. Jimmy was doing *Taxi* and I'm doing *Webster*. We're down the block from each other at the commissary and Jimmy comes by and starts working me. "You had to go to a clicker, huh? What's the matter, you couldn't take it?" I said, "It's pretty sane, Jimmy." Now Jimmy was doing *Taxi*, which was film, he wasn't clicking anything. He gets a tape pilot to do. I'm working *Webster* at the time on the same lot and all of a sudden I get this emergency call from Jimmy Burrows. His fingers have frozen up on him. He asked me if I could come over with my clicker [*laughs*]. Of course I gave him my clicker but the fact was that his fingers froze up. He couldn't snap any longer. He tried the other hand, it was all gone. He lost his snap but that was just an anecdote of that particular period of time. The great clicker moment.

That was what you did. You designed this line cut, shot by shot by shot in your script, you knew that you wanted a line played in a single. You knew you wanted the next line played in a two-shot. You knew you wanted the next line played in the master. You knew that you needed a single of so-and-so for the next shot. The fact was, everything that you wanted was planned out. That was a very good learning experience because you could see everything. You were forced to see, to plan the movie. You're planning the movie shot by shot by shot all while inside the booth.

You would draw a line coming off the end of the line of dialogue in your script where you wanted to cut. Then you'd write the camera letter that's shooting it and the nature of the shot that that camera was shooting.

Meaning camera one, two, three or four. Or A, B, C and X. Then the camera composition of whether it's a one-shot or …

Step 10: Final Shoot

... two-shot or three-shot and you would also have either the first letter of the actor's real name or the character name. If you were shooting a two-shot of CeCe and Rocky, you would write on the line in your script 2s/C & R.

Correct.

Now you're in the booth and you have direct communication with everybody. Mainly the stage manager [title for the assistant director in videotape] through this PL [production line] system. The associate director would be talking directly to the cameramen from the booth based on your marked script.

My audible line feed goes to the camera operators, as well as to the stage manager, as well as to the associate director and the technical director who are sitting with me. The Associate Director sets up the shots. I'm cutting the shots. The TD is taking the cut when I cue it to him, either by snapping or clicking. I think John Tracy used to say, "Bammo!" He nearly took out an associate director at one point. That was a legendary story of how he was just a very emotional cutter and he used it on the big cuts. When he really wanted to time a cut, he used to swing his arms with force.

It was a fun thing to do, to cut shows. I mean, that's what they're doing for the Academy Awards still today. That's what they're doing for *Dancing with the Stars*. That's what they're doing in all of these live shows. A director is in a booth. He's got a plethora of cameras pointing around, doing all kinds of stuff that have been pre-programmed to do things at a different point in a song, or a different point in an interview, or something. Basically, that director is out there viewing monitors and just cutting. Ready one. Take one [*snap*]. Ready two. Take two [*snap*]. Ready three. Take three [*snap*]. All that kind of rhythm that the director develops. There were great directors whose strongest suit was their ability to cut on the fly.

Which was again more stressful and more demanding because you were doing it in this live environment.

Very much so. It was everything from that particular point on that they needed to edit or modify because the performance was based on the line cut and you can be pretty well sure that 90 percent of that line cut was exactly what showed up when they showed it on network TV. You are the voice of

The Booth vs. the Floor

God from the booth. A story I have on *Full House*: I was fed up with some of the actors' behavior and I announced over the P.A. system, hitting this red button creating the voice of God on stage, I was screaming to the floor, "That's it! I've had it with you guys. Everybody in the green room in five minutes!" so I charged to the green room, ready to rip apart Bob Saget, Dave Coulier and John Stamos for some kind of carrying on they were doing. But they brought the little twins with them, and all the girls were sitting there staring up at me pleasantly, while the guys would just be hysterical over the fact I couldn't say anything to them. It was a long walk from the booth, too.

This control booth was either in a van or truck outside or it was behind the audience bleachers, but you were in a confined area. A lot of producers would be in that room and they'd be watching the process.

Usually, if you are lucky, the producers would move into another room, where they did have access to everything that you had, but they weren't sitting behind your back. I've had it both ways. Let me tell you, having them behind you is more unnerving than having them in a different room.

Sure would be. Now they've taken the booth and put in on the floor, creating a satellite situation which we call "Video Village."

I call it "Idiot Village." No offense intended.

This is where there's no more confinement; there's no more walls. Anybody can see the monitors with the four-camera quad split and the line cut. There is a protocol of having the director and the executive producers in the front row along with the network. The communication is now more tangible. You can just run into the set and fix a problem. Do you find that is there is more of an advantage being closer?

There's no question about it. The nature of the business has changed when everybody can look at monitors, and make determinations and anybody can worry about a line reading and make determinations. That's already built into the system. You can't do much about that. What it does help is the fact that the communication between the creative people, who are specifically responsible for the decision-making process, is immediate and right there. The communication to the actors in terms of speaking to them about what it

Step 10: Final Shoot

is we need from them in the next take, or what it is we didn't get from them in the previous take, or a line that they blew to such a degree that we didn't even understand what language they were speaking. These things can now be transmitted really quickly and really efficiently to the process. Like in anything else, you build an organization that learns to work together.

Even on the floor, the director, whoever the executive producer or the spokesman for the producers may be, in the case of *Shake it Up*, we've mentioned Rob Lotterstein, or it could have been anybody else that he chose to have down there on the floor that day, usually another co-executive producer, like Eileen Conn. The communication between myself, that person, and the network person responsible to Disney for what was going on. Those three people have to be heard in terms of every choice that's made.

Now everybody's looking to infuse their opinion on everything that happens. Mostly, it's a question of seeing something that they believe needs being fixed or that didn't quite happen the way they thought it can happen. Maybe we can have an insert there to tell the story better. They may see things in terms of the camera blocking and the shooting where they say, "Wait a second. I'm not seeing the fact that her heels are outrageously long. Is there something we can do to solve that problem?" It just happened recently on a show of ours. CeCe had outrageously long heels. I mean, they could have been eight-inch spikes. The fact was the way she picked them up, they couldn't quite read on camera how big and strange those spikes were. So I said, "Okay, let me try something else." I moved the line to an early part in the scene where I could stand them in a particular place and hold them to get some shots that I wanted, and see the heels at the same time. So I got that problem solved.

The adjustment was easily solved because you were right there on the floor next to the set. It enabled you to run into the set and say, "Okay. Let's do this instead." On the fly. The beauty about something like that is that we're able to keep the cameras rolling because you're that much closer to the set. However, you are losing the privacy factor.

We lost the privacy factor in this industry years ago. The day somebody put $1 in for something that they were involved in, they wanted $1 worth of input. However, if I can solve a problem that they seem to have, I will be able to jump in faster and try to solve the problem. And with my years of doing this, I sometimes have a pretty good shot at fixing it. If sometimes a joke isn't working at the end of a scene, then that's usually the writers responsibility and they'll come up to me and they'll say, "What do you think of these two lines?" I will immediately say, "Oh, go with the first line," and immediately they'll do that first line.

A lot of times, restaging something helps get the right delivery of a line.
That could very well be, but by that point when I'm shooting, if I have that much restaging to do, I shouldn't be hired to do the job, to be quite honest.

What system did you like better, the booth or the floor?
I love the floor. I love being with the actors. If I had to define myself, I'd define myself as an actor's director and being on the floor puts me in closer proximity to them and that's what I love most about it.

The Director's Cut

So now we've finished shooting. Whether it's with or without an audience show, you have everything you feel you needed to create the product that you were given to create. What happens next, with regards to the director's cut and everything that happens in post-production?
Essentially, all that material, which is now on high-def, is transferred directly to the editing room and the editor, with the help of the script notes and the assistant editor assembles the first cut, the editor's cut, a complete assemblage of the entire episode, trying to determine for himself what he thinks the director would've liked and, in certain instances, if they've worked together long enough, they're probably going to be pretty much on the same page. Anyway, I will receive an editor's cut.

Tell us more about the script notes and the editing process.
The script supervisor will mark how many takes of a scene happened and there is going to be something different in each take. But it's the producers and the director on the floor, although I don't get into it myself, but I know

Step 10: Final Shoot

that the director certainly has a right to be into it, will choose which were the best takes. If I do three takes of a scene and we determine that the first half of the scene was brilliant in take one, but we got to play the entire second part of the scene from take three, well, then that's going to go up to the editor. He'll have those notes and he will try to put together the episode based on those notes.

He'll do it to a high percentage, but if he sees something as he's editing that looks strange to him in what came up from the floor, so to speak, in these notes, he may not worry about it. He may just cut it the way he feels was the best performance rather than necessarily adhering to the script notes because, to be quite honest, the vision on the floor is sometimes tainted. It's tainted as to what the best take is. When you start to look at them in post, you may realize that the take you thought was so great on the floor, that third take that was the golden take, and you start to look at it on screen and now it looks overacted. Something looks strange to you about the take that you did not see when it was being performed and you go back and you make those adjustments if you need to. Then what happens is, I get the editor's version and I create my notes based on that version. Could you go to this camera instead of that camera? Can you do this instead of that?

I will even make suggested dialogue cuts or little snippets of scene cuts if the piece is going to need to be cut. I will not take those cuts. I will simply have the editor mark down what the director suggests because I know the producers like to hear all their words. They want to see all the words that they wrote on screen and then worry about the five minutes that they're too long, but I'll only make suggestions for length cuts. That's not your responsibility.

When I get in the room with the editor, we will go through it scene by scene and I will point out the shots that I thought we would use that we didn't use. I might point out something, I'll go, "Wait a second. I don't like that performance. Do we have something in take one?, I think I remember something in take one..." and I will actually go back on something that may have been said on the floor and I'll create my vision of what's called the director's cut.

After me, there's much more work to be done. Now the producers get their hands on it and the producers have their responsibility which is to get it down to time, so if they're three or four minutes too long, they're going to have to cut. They're helped usually by the network correspondent who sees

The Director's Cut

these cuts that the producer is making and will suggest areas that the network would like to see trimmed and areas that the network really doesn't want you to trim. The executive producer and the network go through a big negotiating process and then the final cut comes out.

Then there's sound mixing that has to be done. We may have to do some ADR [automated dialogue replacement] work. We may have to do some looping. We may have to do any number of things to finish off the package. There might be some scoring that's done for the show that has to be put in. Essentially that work is all post and, for the most part, once I finish my director's cut, that's the last time I deal with that episode. To be quite honest, you'd be wise to just get it out of your head that you're going to have any more input. However, I watch all the shows on the air. I watch the air versions and, you know something, I am to a great degree very happy with the shows that they're turning out. They usually manage to look very similar to my director's cut. Maybe some pieces are missing because they had to do some editing that I wasn't doing. They tightened it, they've added some laughs, they added some reaction shots, and for the most part I think that nine times out of ten they made the shows better.

I agree because they actually have more time to ...
To play and to think.

Conclusion

In this chapter, Joel discusses the long term rewards of directing sitcoms. The unique and gratifying opportunity to build wonderful relationships that can last a lifetime. Joel explains all the benefits of working in this medium and how it is the best job in the world.

Making Comedy Fun: The Life of a Sitcom Director

If you can't make doing comedy fun, you're in the wrong business. It is the greatest job in the world, to go to work every day and laugh because people are trying to be funny, because writers are writing funny jokes …

And get paid for it.
And you're getting paid for it. It's so crazy. I mean, I started out, I got my Master in Commedia dell'Arte. Then I went to work at La MaMa, an experimental theater in New York with Tom O'Horgan there, Jerzy Grotowski there, Peter Brooke there. It was a phenomenal incubator place. *Godspell* and *Hair* were created at La MaMa. It was a bastion of avant garde theater and I went from La MaMa to *Laverne & Shirley*. People are going, "How do you do that? How does that even happen?" I said, "Well, I saw *Laverne & Shirley* and I thought all this was commedia." Commedia are stock characters who are put in stock situations that the audience knows. They love the characters and they love to see them in these situations. How many times do you do the same kind of a show, episode by episode? The cabin show or the diet pill show or in some other version of those shows. They keep on repeating their stock situations. They always say they only have seven stories to tell. But the fact is, once I address sitcom as commedia, my whole background seems to fit just

nicely. I had no problem from that particular point on. It's the best job in the world. Listen, it was three weeks on, one week off; two weeks off for Christmas, three months off for hiatus. Get a couple of pilots, okay, so you had two months off for hiatus. That's an enormous amount of time not to have to be working and have income that's carrying you through that period of time because of residuals and because of whatever it is that you get because of the pay that they give to directors, it's fairly remarkable. I was able to raise my kids, go to swimming meets with Jamie, go to karate competitions with Hillary, be part of raising my kids while I was doing this. Both kids, Hillary and Jamie, did seven or eight episodes of *Full House*. Every time Jody Sweeten had a classroom scene, she always knew where she sat, right next to Hillary [*laughs*]. Hillary would be sitting there and Jody would say, "I guess that's my seat." I said yes, because if you're not in that seat, you may not be in the shot because Hillary's getting in the shot. And Jamie is sitting right behind them. I was able to raise my kids while raising actor kids on *Full House* and laughing and making money. It was insane. I came from doing La MaMa where I got a stipend. Ellen Stewart, the La MaMa herself, gave me a stipend of $50 a week cash, which was amazing. It was unbelievably good money. Fifty a week cash is what I got for quite a few years at La MaMa. If I made more than $2500 a year, I was having myself a good year. Then I come to Hollywood and the beginning salary back in 1978 for directing a half-hour sitcom—this was just base salary—was $5000 for an episode. I didn't make $5000 in the previous two years. The whole thing is mind-boggling in terms of the amount of money people were paying to do this job. I thought, "Wow, this is cool. I can deal with this."

What do you love about sitcoms?

What I love the most about situation comedies is, I get to work every day and I get to laugh because what we're trying to do is be funny. If you're a director, you are the audience that the actors first run into as they try this material out and if you're laughing and having a great ol' time with their choices, I think you're ahead of the game. What I also like about the sitcom is the fact that it's only a week of your life. In one week it can be the greatest show you've ever done or it could be a turkey but it's over in one week and you get to go in again on another episode with new challenges, with new problems to solve. It's a problem-solving venue, how to make the story work, how to make the jokes work, how to make gags work, how to make special effects work. These are problems that have to be solved.

We have isolated a weekly rundown of how you must attack these things when their time comes. There used to be a commercial about, "We will sell no wine before its time." Well, essentially you have to time the process. You want to get everything ready for when that camera rolls. You want the best performance the actor ever gave in front of the lens. You want it all to happen there. Therefore, your job is to lead yourself up to that, to ramp up to that. You don't want to blow yourself out on the greatest Tuesday run-through in history, only to find the show disintegrating on Wednesday, and by the time you're shooting on Thursday and Friday they're bored with it. You have to emotionally guide an episode. I like that.

In the case of what I'm doing now, I love working with kids. I did it my entire career. I fell into it starting with *Full House* and *Family Matters* and *Step by Step* and now *Shake It Up* and kids are great. They don't have egos, they're wide-eyed, they're open-faced, they want to try hard and you're not getting much ego out of them which is terrific. It takes an enormous amount of pressure off of dealing with actors. I just love watching them grow up off-camera, watching them grow up on- camera, watching little 13-year-old girls leave me when they're 17 as young women and that's mind boggling. I've raised three daughters of my own and a son, so I know the process, but it forever intrigues me. It just forever intrigues me as they grow up in those really critical years they're between, let's say about 11, 12 and 17. If you're lucky enough to be with them during that growth period, you benefit greatly, you learn as a human being. It's probably the thing that keeps me happiest right now.

You're like a surrogate parent to these kids.

Probably because of my age, I'm more of a surrogate grandparent because I think I'm a surrogate parent to their parents. I care. I'm interested in who so-and-so's boyfriend is. Will you bring him down to the set? I want to meet this guy. And it turns out he's a nice guy and I let her know, I say, "Hey, he's a really nice guy, I like him, he's very cool." And I want to know what they're about. I need to know what's going on. I want to know what they're schooling is like. I am very heavily involved in how well they're doing in school. I gave up my personal dressing room so they could have an additional schoolroom because I wanted the kids to have the best education possible and it's working. These kids are bright, they're educated, they work hard in school, they're motivated, and I feel really good about that. I thought we did great with the *Full House* kids too. Jaleel White, the star of *Family Matters*, is a UCLA college graduate, super-bright. We have done very well, in my years, working with kids in terms of letting them be kids and at the same time having them grow up with you on camera.

It's a different kind of energy to deal with and certainly not an energy to be afraid of. Is there a downside?

The big downside of sitcom is that as a visionary, as somebody who would like to be able to tell a more complicated story, visually you're not going to get that in sitcom for the most part.

You figured out the system and how to work it, not just milk it, but work it in the most effective way that a sitcom director can. I used to watch you and say to myself, "Wow, Joel is handling this differently than I would. He's figured it out." Tell me if you've always been this way or is this also something learned? How do you know when to give input, when to say things that you need to say, and when to step aside and let the other people do the work?

Some of that has to do with just who I am. I was always the systems kid. I always saw that there was a system in doing something and I always wanted to get into the system and make the system work more efficiently. That's just how my brain went. The rest of it is just a question of years in the business. Craft keeps growing. You see the game, the game is being played slower in front of your eyes, just like they say sometimes for a basketball player, the game has slowed down. And despite the fact that everybody's running at a mad pace for you, you're seeing the bloody game in slow motion. Well, I'm seeing what we're doing in slow motion because I trained myself to see so fast that essentially it's slow motion for me. I can get work done in a millisecond that would take five minutes for other people discussing what needs to get done. A lot of that has to do with years that they let me work and I got better and better. I got more social. I got politically smarter. I had some strange run-ins at the beginning of my career because I was an irascible man who would be short-tempered and could get really questionable in terms of behavior.

I was lucky in that people thought enough of my talent to let me get away with some of those really stupid things I did in my early directing career. I had backers. I had Bob Boyette and Tom Miller who protected me and who felt that I gave an energy to their shows that they thought was terrific and they wanted me, so they basically protected me from myself until I got smart enough to get out of my own way. But then again, I always say, we're lucky to survive our youth. There's so many stupid things we can do in our youth and I'm one of the lucky ones who survived it and learned from it and kept learning. I think that anybody who's been around in a creative career will say the same thing, that they are better today than they were when they started out. Somebody's got to give you a chance to keep doing it and you'll get better and if you're suited for it, catch a couple of lucky breaks, you can get it done.

You also know when to say yes, which is 90 percent of the time, to the executive producers, and when to say no. Even if it goes against what you think it's supposed to be, you managed to be able to make it work for everybody by saying, "Yes, I'll make it work," and then you figure it out. You figure out a way to satisfy the request.

I know the parameters of what it can be and therefore I have taken a choice that I felt was the legitimate choice at solving a problem. But I've been through permutations of combinations of how else to solve the problem and I just thought the way I chose was the best way to solve it. Then the writers come up to me, or the producer, and say, "You know, it'd be much better if we didn't stop them at the table and let them go right into the living room." And I said, "But you got a line there that seems to indicate they're stopping." And the producer will go, "Well, then, I'll just get rid of the line," and we'll solve the problem that way.

I tracked it through my head, at that point I knew I had a big funny line happening. I had to stop them someplace. I had to do something and the producers would rather have it fly in so they had to restructure a little bit of the writing so it became an apparently better solution to the solving of the staging problem of a moment. Basically the only way you can see the movie you wish to make is by seeing much of the movie that you don't want to make. You go through the choices and you say, "Well, if I do this, this and this…. No, no, if I do that, I'm not going to like that because I don't want that to happen." Therefore, "If I do this, this, this and this, well, now that makes more sense but, if I do this, this, this and that, yeah, of all those choices, that's the best choice." And that's what I'll start to work from, but I've been through all the other possibilities so that if an idea comes up, if an objection comes up, I can switch on a dime. I used to say to myself that I had the integrity of a weather vane.

And that's what Frank Pace said to me: "Do yourself a favor and watch how Joel says yes to everything the network and producers ask."

Yeah, everything is yes. And every once in a while I'll go up to an executive producer and I'll say, "Watch out for that moment if I were you." I will never do it to embarrass the producers or to look like I'm getting into some kind of a war with the writer-producers or the network. No, I can make anything work and if they come up with something that I have questions about, I will speak to them directly and say, "Are you sure you want this, guys? Because if you do that, you're going to live on the back end with A, B and C," and they'll go, "Oh, yeah, you're right. Okay, then let's not do that." I mean, if that's what you're going to base your career on is saying, "No, you're not getting that single. I don't want to see that single in my show…." Well you can't do that.

Would you say that directors can benefit from training in other fields?

I didn't plan on being a director. I had no goals to be a director. I didn't study to be a director particularly. I took some quick courses in speech and theater and some early TV production courses, but that wasn't because I thought I was going to be a director, I didn't know what I was going to be. I graduated with a B.A. in Brooklyn College with no goals, so I worked for the Bureau of Child Welfare, then I went to Berkeley when some friends said, "Hey, come to Berkeley with us," and that didn't work out for me very well. Then I went back to Brooklyn and little by little my life started to shape up and then one day I found myself in a position to direct and it worked, it was a success. *The Last Chance Saloon* played the West End of London and I traveled through Europe with the play and I became a director. Now, I was the director of La MaMa Plexus, where I directed a few more productions including one that my buddy, Greg Antonacci acted in. He was the same guy from *Busting Loose*, talk about connections in a business, he joined my company in New York. He wrote a musical called *Dance with Me*. Played Broadway for a year, got me a Tony nomination, got me a Drama Desk nomination, and then all of a sudden this guy Stephan Slane, who owned and produced a summer stock theater, Cape Cod Melody Tent, wanted to take a meeting with me.

Did you direct Dance with Me?

Yes. I directed, choreographed and co-starred. It was just an ensemble of lunatics from La MaMa who made their way onto Broadway. Then all of a sudden the next level happened to me, Stephan Slane. I go into his office and he says, "I've been watching your career now for a few years." I go, "What? You've been watching my career?" I didn't know I had a career. He's watching my career and he says, "I'd like to hire you to direct some touring musicals for me this summer." I went on to direct John Raitt and Howard Keel in *Shenandoah* and Christine Andreas in *Oklahoma!* and then somebody else got me involved with a project called *Merry-Go-Round*, a musical revue, and it played a year in Chicago and I got a production in Las Vegas.

So, I'm in Las Vegas putting up *Merry-Go-Round* at some hotel there, a downtown hotel. After putting up the show, I had a couple of weeks free and thought, "Wow, I'll go out to L.A. I've never been to L.A., I'm only an hour away, I'll go visit with Greg," who at that time was already doing *Busting Loose* as a writer and as a co-star. I came out and at that time I think he was living with Annie Potts, so I stayed with them and that was when Greg got in his brain that I should direct an episode of *Busting Loose*. Lowell Ganz and Mark Rothman, the exec producers of the show, also went to Queens College when I taught there. That's why Greg was out in Hollywood, they dragged him out. They knew who I was because they knew of my classes at Queens College because they were legendary, hundreds of kids tumbling on lawns. My class consisted of only 20 kids, but hundreds of kids showed up in these classes just having a ball tumbling around and doing improvisational games or whatever I was teaching at that particular time. I did my episode of *Busting Loose* and it was a successful episode. I went back to New York, my home, and I was directing an Off Broadway play called *Esther* based on the Purim legend and then I noticed in the papers that Mark Rothman and Lowell Ganz were going to be exec-producing a brand new series for Ted Knight, who had just come off *The Mary Tyler Moore Show*. It was going to be called *The Ted Knight Show*. So I wrote them saying, "Hey, listen, if there's any chance I can get to direct for you guys again, I'd sure love to come out and do that." And sure enough, they invited me out to direct an episode and from there I started working.

Separating Your Style from the System

I want to make it clear in all of what I've been talking about is how to separate style from system. That's what we're trying to elucidate here, a system of how a half-hour sitcom is most efficiently put together. What I'm not trying to do here is determine what style it is that you bring to the system. Whether your strengths are in working with actors, whether your strengths are in visualization and use of camera, whether your strengths are organizational, whether your strengths are deductive, inductive, I don't care what that's about, one has to still develop a system for the style that you employ and that system has to be as efficient as possible because the TV sitcom world demands efficiency. You cannot be sitting around taking long times to make decisions.

In the final analysis I think that the director of a sitcom, more than anything else, has to make decisions. You are the top of the heap. You must make a decision, and it's not important initially whether your decision is the best or not the best, it will start the decision-making process. Now everybody who works with you can input on your decision, but if you don't make a decision, people are just standing around waiting for a decision to be made. That's a big waste of time. As you get more involved in the business, hopefully more of your decisions will become good ones, but the fact is, it doesn't make a difference, you still have to make the decisions. Decision-making is the critical aspect to directing a sitcom.

Style is judged. Basically, if you have a wonderful style and you envision phenomenal shooting patterns and all kinds of stuff that are off the charts, it doesn't help you unless you get the job done. You have to be sure that the style you're employing actually tells a story. Usually in sitcom, the story is very much told from an audience point of view. You're watching characters do something and it's not from a camera point of view where you might be seeing the actor's point of view. You might shoot down on them, you might shoot up on them, you might be walking with them seeing what they are seeing, which are decidedly camera point of view shots. We do a little bit of it in sitcoms and sometimes they're critical because a specific story necessitates a specific kind of shot, which is not necessarily an audience point of view shot but maybe a high angle looking down at this world, or it might be a low angle looking up at somebody. These are valuable shots that have to be judiciously employed.

And that's pretty much what I wanted to make sure we established. No right or wrong about style but you've got to be efficient. Adapt the system that basically works for your style because we understand that every director is different and every director brings a slightly different bent or impulse to the work and you have to go with your strengths as a director but, at the same time, be prepared to understand the nature of the business.

I said earlier that we build craft as we get a chance to work longer and longer in the business. That notwithstanding, you must operate based on the craft you currently have. No matter what that level of craft is, it could be simply coming out of film school. It could be simply directing a play Off Broadway. That's your level of craft, you will bring that to the table and you will work within that level. But that's no reason not to produce some of the best work of your life right at the beginning. Tom Hanks has said to me more than once that some of his best work was *Bosom Buddies*. Well that was made with a 21-year-old who just was getting himself wet in this business. Now look at the craft this man has amassed over the last 30 years in films, now on stage. Well, the fact remains that he was able to use his craft base when he was 21 years old to produce the work he did on *Bosom Buddies*. He now uses his craft base as he's closing in on 55 years old to be able to do the work that he wishes to do. Which also applies to you as a director.

That's pretty much it.

Glossary

The Abby Singer Shot: the next-to-last shot of the day while filming or taping. Abby Singer was an assistant director who was known for announcing, "This one and one more."

ADR [Automated dialogue replacement] (Also known as "looping"): When an actor replaces his original dialogue to picture in a synchronized process in post-production due to an unintelligible condition or change in dialogue.

Aspect Ratio: the ratio of the width to the height of an image on screen.

Associate Director (also known as Camera Coordinator): assists the director's technical vision by communicating the director's shots to the camera operators and making adjustments during the camera blocking process. Also readies the cameras for their upcoming shots over the Production Line during actual shooting.

b.g.: an abbreviation for background which describes either "extras" (performers) or the location where some action may be taking place in a shot.

Booth: an designated area usually divided into separate rooms with monitors allowing the technical departments such as Sound and Video to perform their work.

Buddy comedy: a pairing of two friends that have contrasting personalities. A relationship that grows stronger as they encounter life events or situations together.

Bump: a part of the script that doesn't seem to work affecting the reader's flow of the story.

camera block: when you frame or line-up shots through the lens with the actors or stand-ins while rehearsing a scene for the purpose of shooting.

Camera Coordinator: see Associate director

Cheat: when an actor performs in a manner that is not consistent with the original blocking to make the shot work better in front of the camera.

Glossary

Check the Gate: ensuring that the gate in the camera where the film passes through is clean of hair, dust and other particles.

Child Labor Laws: state laws that govern the employment of minors.

Chuffa: added continued dialogue (to be recorded separately and used in post-production) for an actor that is giving a speech or talking to others in a scene as the scene jumps to other actors in another part of the set. We may or may not see the original actor in the background of the shot with the other actors but we will hear this continued dialogue in the background in the final cut of the scene.

Clapperboard: a blackboard that provides information for each shot: title of show or movie, name of the director, the director of photography, the scene and take numbers, date, and time. It's filmed at the beginning of every take and the hinged clapper is audibly snapped shut to provide picture and sound synchronization for post-production editing.

Clean: refers to an actor being shot alone in a frame as opposed to having another actor visible within the frame.

Clearing the Eye-Line: minimizing visual distractions for the actors.

Clicker: a small clicking device used by directors to signal to the video switcher to cut to the next shot in the director's line cut while directing in the booth. This device is rarely used in situation comedies anymore.

Close-up: a shot that is tight enough to capture the emotions of an actor's face, or the details of set pieces or props.

Cold Opening: the first scene of a script, that sets up the story and usually runs before opening credits.

Commedia dell'Arte: improvised performances by a stock troupe of actors based on sketches or scenarios.

Condor: a mobile stand that is used on set to position lights or cameras in the air, and to facilitate stunts and special effects.

Cover Set: an interior set that is made available for future use, when inclement weather forces a scheduled exterior day to be moved inside.

Coverage: footage beyond the traditional master shot using various lens sizes and different angles to provide the editor with more choices when cutting a scene.

Cowboy Shot: a shot framed from just below the waist, where a cowboy's holster would be. A throwback to Westerns.

Glossary

Craft Service: the department that is responsible for supplying food and beverages to the working crew and also responsible for stage or set cleanup.

Crane Shot: taken with a camera housed on the extended arm of a crane, which provides height and fluid motion. It is typically used for high angle shots above the set and to capture the master shot of a scene.

C-stand: a metal stand with various arms and clamps allowing objects to be held at various heights and angles in order to optimize lighting.

Curtain call: When the cast is brought out for a final bow after a live performance.

Dance floor: usually a ¾ inch thick piece of plywood covered with masonite to provide a smooth surface for the dollying of a camera.

Day for Night: to shoot a scene that takes place at night during the day.

Day out of Days: refers to how many days in the shooting schedule a particular actor has agreed to work. This number is often discussed during negotiations for the actors' services.

Director's Cut: usually the first edited cut of a project, put together by the editor with notes and input only from the director.

Dirty: a shot where an extraneous character or object is visible, although focus is on another character or object.

Disney Death: the temporary death of an animated character who then miraculously comes back to life.

Director of Photography: the crew member responsible for composing shots and setting the lights.

Do-si-do: to ask two actors to switch spots or to turn the camera around and shoot in the opposite direction. Taken from the square-dancing term.

Downstage: the part of the set that is closest to the audience or camera side of a set. The term was coined from theater stages that were slightly slanted moving upwards towards the back of the stage in order to help the audience see the actors better when standing in back of the stage. So, if an actor was walking toward the audience they were actually moving downstage.

Dress to Camera: to place objects or characters within the frame, so that they are visible through the camera.

Dry run: when the crew watches a rehearsal of the staged blocking of a scene with actors prior to camera blocking.

Dub: to tape over the original audio recording of a project.

Glossary

Duvetyne: a heavy black cloth which is used by the grip department to black out windows, diffuse light, and hide or protect equipment.

Elephant Doors: big stage doors that electrically open and close to provide access to the set for large set pieces, animals and equipment.

Executive Producer: also known as the "show runner." The head writer who is generally responsible for delivery of the final product. Has direct input relating to all aspects of filming required to achieve the end result. In television the executive producer is often a show's creator.

Extras: background actors who help fill out a scene.

Fifty-Fifty: a camera shot in which two actors face each other and take up an equal amount of the camera frame.

Final-Cut: the version of the film that will be released to the general public.

First Team: refers to the principal actors who will work in front of the camera, as compared to stand-ins or stunt doubles, who are referred to as the second team.

Fish Pole: a long pole with a microphone at the end of it used to record dialog or other sound.

Flag: a device used to control and direct light. Usually the material is in a metal frame.

Fly in: get something to the set in an expedited manner.

Foreground cutting piece: any object or set piece strategically placed in the set to fill a void in the bottom portion of a frame.

4:3: An old square viewing aspect ratio for television screens. Still used in some International television broadcasts.

Gack: a term used for crew working material, tools or equipment.

Gaffer: the head of the electrical / lighting department. Responsible for the execution, and sometimes design, of a production's lighting plan.

"Go on a bell and roll": what the assistant director says to the sound mixer in the booth when the director is ready to shoot a scene. The traditional stage bell rings which notifies everyone in earshot that the cameras are now rolling and to refrain from talking during the take until the director yells "cut" at which time you will hear another bell signifying that the cameras have stopped rolling and you can resume talking. A Red light usually found above the stage doors will coincide with the bell so you don't exit or enter the stage during this time.

Glossary

Golden Hour: when the sun rises or sets and exterior light is at its prettiest. Also known as Magic Hour.

Good eyes: a term used when you see both eyes of an actor in a shot.

Greek: a word, sequence of words or a logo distorted so that it does not appear in its original form.

Grip: crew member who's responsible for camera and electrical equipment.

Gurney: a cart used by the grips and electricians.

Haircut: the framing of an actor's face that cuts off part of the top of the head or hair.

Handheld: a camera operated manually, without the support of a tripod or a dolly, allowing for greater freedom of motion but risking a shakier shot.

Hero: an object (possibly a prop or piece of set dressing) that is the main focus of a shot or scene.

Hiatus: the period of time (usually a week) during production that there is no shooting. This gives the writers time to produce more scripts and production to prepare or complete episodes on the schedule.

"Hold it": a term used to stop all action whether it be cast or crew.

HMI *(Hydrargyrum Medium-Arc Iodide)* **Light:** popular lighting for on-set filming because the rays of the arc lamp create the effect of sunlight.

Honeywagon: a production vehicle used to house actors, extras, often the assitant director's onset office, as well as restrooms.

"In the Can": refers to a project or scene which has been shot but not necessarily developed or edited. May also be used when a project's photography has been completed.

Insert: a close-up or cutaway shot used to provide detail or highlight a plot point. Could be words on a page, a ring, a hand turning off a light, keys, etc.

International Alliance of Theatrical Stage Employees (IATSE): the labor union to which almost all crew members on union projects belong.

Introductions: When the cast is introduced to an audience before shooting a live show.

Jib Arm: a counterweighted piece of equipment used to hold a camera for an increased range of motion, perhaps to move the camera over water or a table or above a crowd.

Kicker: usually a hard light used to highlight features or detail: cheekbones, lips, a tattoo, etc.

"Knock it Down": take the shine or luster off of something. Either because light is bouncing off the object and causing a glare on camera or to add age to its appearance.

"Last Looks": an alert from the assistant director to make up, hair and wardrobe personnel that filming will be begin soon, so the actors and set should be given a final once-over.

Layout Board: cardboard floor cover used to protect the floor from wear and tear on a set.

Line cut: the rough chronological version of a show based on the director's marked script that is created live by a video switcher during shooting.

Location Scout: someone who visits potential locations prior to filming to decide the best place to shoot the project.

Lock-Off: to secure a camera in place so that continuous takes are exactly the same. Often used to film an effect or time lapse.

Looping: see ADR

Lunch: any meal break taken during the shooting day.

"Make a Meal of It": an instruction for an actor or camera operator to really get into a scene. Encouragement to go overboard.

Make the Day: to complete all of the scenes and work that you had planned on at the start of the day.

Mark: a piece of tape or other device used to let actors know where their feet or other body part should be. Also used to mark the location of furniture or other set pieces, so that if they are moved they are replaced in the correct spot.

Martini: the last shot of the day following the Abbey Singer shot. A warning called out by the assistant director to prepare the crew that the work day is about to end.

Master Shot: a wide shot that usually covers the entire scene and all of its elements.

Matching: the process of lining up what happens in one shot with the next so that the action looks continuous.

Medium: a shot that is framed from around the belt-line of an actor.

Mix: the blending of all of the audio elements of a project.

Moiré pattern: a distorted look on camera from an actor's wardrobe with a designed pattern that has closely spaced stripes or other designs. The director of photography will request that the wardrobe is changed before shooting.

Glossary

MOS (Motor only sync): to record a scene without recording audio.

Most Favored Nations Clause: a contract clause that states that the individual will be treated as well as any other individual doing the same job function, in regard to matters such as credits, profit participation, dressing rooms, etc.

N.G.: a take or shot that is not usable or No Good.

"Need Better eyes": a term used when you want to see both eyes of an actor in a shot.

Noncombatants: those who are not involved in the current scene.

Obie: a small light mounted on the camera just above the lens, used to highlight an actor's facial features.

One-er: a scene shot in one continuous take, often with a steadicam or handheld camera so the cameraman can shoot and follow the action. The TV show *ER* often used a one-er to highlight the drama of the emergency room.

One for Safety: shooting a scene or shot an additional time in case something went awry in the previous take.

180 degree rule: an imaginary line that creates an axis of action between actors and the camera. The camera must not cross the line or it would reverse the direction of the scene.

Open up: a request made by the director or cameraman for the actors to turn towards the camera so their eyes or other features are more visible.

Over: a camera shot shooting over the back or shoulder of one character and looking at an object or another character. Used to establish the geography of the characters or objects.

PA system: (public announcement system) the way a director communicates to the floor from the booth via a loud speaker system. Used during camera blocking, pre-shooting or live audience shows.

Pan: to turn the camera from one side to another along its own axis either establishing a set or to follow an actor or action.

Pedestal or (Ped): the mobile traditional video camera support with a viewfinder. The ped enables the camera to move up, down, left and right. The camera can also be raised up to 8 ft or more for shooting high angles. The camera operators also have the ability to change focus and the composition of a shot via a switch on the arms of the ped.

Perms: the walkways above the sets towards the roof of the stage.

Glossary

Pick Points: a designated area where cables are hung for special effects or stunts.

Pickup: to continue a shot or scene somewhere after its original start point.

Piece of Business: action by a character to help him look engrossed in what he is doing, i.e., adjusting his tie, counting his money, taking a drink, etc.

Pilot: the very first episode that is given more time and money to shoot to be considered for a network series pick-up.

Practical: a light on a set that is seen on camera and is part of the set. Could be a desk light, a chandelier, a bedroom lamp, etc.

Producer: the main producer is generally responsible for the hiring of the key crew members and making sure the project is completed on budget and on time. The producer also acts as a liaison between the director, executive producer, the actors, and the network, studio and/or production company.

Production Designer: the crew member responsible for the overall artistic look of a production.

Production Line or (PL): a wireless and private communication line from the director, associate director or assistant director to the crew via headsets.

Proscenium: the part of the stage that is in front of the set or action of a scene. The proscenium can change throughout a scene therefore creating camera resets to accommodate the new location of the action.

"Put it on its feet": when the director starts to rehearse the script with the actors on set.

Ritters: large fans that are used to create strong winds.

Room Tone: ambient sound that is recorded on an interior or exterior set and later may be incorporated by the sound editors into the audio mix.

Rough Cut: the first edited version of a project, which helps to give the director and editor an idea of what elements might be missing.

Sandbags: used on set to stabilize lighting and photography equipment.

Scratch track or Temp Dub: a temporary soundtrack made up of a preliminary mix of dialogue, music, and sound effects, so that early footage may be viewed with all of these elements incorporated.

Script Supervisor: responsible for the timing and the tracking of the individual scenes, shots and takes. Keeps continuity notes, assists actors with dialog as needed and serves as a liaison between the writers and the set crew.

Set: the area where a scene will be shot. Can be interior or exterior, on

Glossary

a stage, or at a location. It is designed by the production designer or art director and decorated and furnished by the set crew.

Show and tell: When department heads, usually props, set dressing, special effects & wardrobe show their work to the executive producer, director and sometimes network executive for choices &/or progress.

Showcard: a piece of white cardboard used as a light reflector.

Sides: a 5:7 version of the day's work, excerpted from the script and distributed each morning to cast and crew.

Single: a shot containing only one actor.

16:9: An aspect ratio which is the standard rectangular viewing format for television screens.

Smash cut: where one scene abruptly cuts to another for an aesthetic or narrative purpose.

Sound Mixer: the crew member responsible for recording all audio during production.

Soundstage: a large soundproof building used for filming. Sets, office space for the crew and audience seating (if necessary) are constructed within the soundstage.

Special Effects Coordinator: the person in charge of building, creating and executing special effects. Will usually run a required safety meeting before the effect takes place.

Speed: an announcement from the sound mixer that the audio recording has begun and an alert for actors to begin performing once the director calls for action.

Spill: when light falls where it is not intended to.

Split Looks: when a character is talking to two or more people and it appears that they are not looking in the right direction.

Squibs: small explosive packets used to look like a bullet hitting a person or object.

Stage Direction: The action of a scene written in the script that explains what, where, how and when an actor performs either dialogue or physical action. Also, may describe a set for better visualization of a scene.

Stand-In: closely resembles an actor and physically represents the character by mimicking the action before shooting to help the crew work on and perfect lighting and camera moves.

Glossary

Steadicam: a stabilized camera that is hand held and used to help shots look fluid and continuous. Very helpful when shooting one-ers.

Stunt Coordinator: the person in charge of choreographing all aspects of any stunt in a scene. He also hires and assigns stunt performers to execute the stunts and spearheads all safety measures for his crew and any actor that may be performing a stunt.

Stunt Double: a stunt performer hired to take the place of an actor in order to perform a dangerous stunt. Usually hired to look like the actor.

Sweeten: to add sound or music to a previously existing audio track.

Tag: a short scene at the end of a script that usually has some kind of upbeat ending for the show.

Tech Scouting: once the locations are chosen, this is a trip to tour them with key department heads, so all can make a plan for shooting.

Tilt: an up or down movement of the camera on its own axis.

Trailer: a tightly edited 1–3 minute highlight of selected shots from the project.

Treatment: used within the motion picture industry as selling documents to outline story and character aspects of a planned screenplay.

Two-shot: the inclusion of two actors in one shot.

Two Ts: shooting an actor from their chest up.

Upstage: the part of the set that is further away from the audience or camera side of a set.

Video Village: a collection of director's chairs and a monitor so that the director, script supervisor, executives, and producers can watch a live feed.

Walk Away: a command by the assistant director for all except the actors to exit the set.

Walla: the sound of many voices talking at the same time.

Wrangler: a person in charge of supervising a large group of extras, or a term used for animal trainers.

Wrap: the end of the shooting day.

The Zone: an area near the particular city in which a union crew lives. If shooting happens outside of the zone then it is considered on location and certain financial accommodations must be met.

INDEX

Numbers in bold italics indicate pages with photographs.

Abdul-Jabbar, Kareem 135–136
Academy Awards 2, 63, 142
Actor's studio 63
ad libs 61
ADR (automated dialogue replacement) 147
Allen, Gary 48
Allen, Woody 16
Andreas, Christine 155
animals 78–80
Antonacci, Greg 9–10, 155
Any Given Sunday 20
Arkin, Adam 9
Arnaz, Desi 107, 139–140
Arney, Randall 63
art department 35
assistant director 3, 18, 26, 50, 142
associate director 15, 140, 142
audience 3, 7–8, 36, 43, 68, 74, 87, 90, 105, 107, 116, 119, 124–126, 133–135, 138–139, 143, 145, 149–150, 156–157; point of view 126; show 7–8, 133–135, 139
Austin & Ally 137

Babe 45
"back-staging" 14
Bailey, Ainsley 69; *see also* Garcia, Dina
Baker, Leigh-Allyn 25
Ball, Lucille 133, 139
Barone, Anita 53, 55; *see also* Jones, Georgia
Berkeley (college) 154
"best eyes" 105

"better eyes" 104
Bickley, Bill 39; Bickley-Warren 40
Bleckner, Jeff 17
blocking 1, 5, 47, 60, 85, 96, 98, *113*, 133; *see also* camera blocking
Blue, Rocky 38, 53, 80, 93, 106, 132; *see also* Zendaya
blue revised table draft 7, 47, 50–51, 60, 95; *see also* revisions
Blumenthal, Larry 127
body language 69, 121, 125
Bosom Buddies 1–3, 20, 23, 56–57, 61, 131, 139–140, 157
Boyett, Bob 23, 153; *see also* Miller-Boyett
Brooke, Peter 149
Brooklyn College 65, 154
Brooks, Mel 16
Bryant, Kobe 137
Bryant, Vanessa 137
buddy comedies 56–57, 61, 65
Bureau of Child Welfare 154
Burrows, Jimmy 107, 141

camera blocking 7–8, 13, 16–17, 22, 90, 95, 98, 120–122, 144
camera coordinator 13, 15, 25, 120, 126, 128
camera left 74, 105, *108*
camera meeting 140
camera operators 25, 34, 48, 74, 107, 127, 140, 142
camera positions *94*, *99*, *102–103*, *110*, *114*; placement *117–118*
camera resets 106; *see also* resets
camera right 105, *108*, *114*
camera shots 11
Cameron, Candace 67
Cape Cod Melody Tent 155
Carousel 54
"the carry" 117
carry shot 100–101, 117, 121–122
casting director 23–24, 39
CGI (computer-generated imagery) 33
Chandler, Tyson 138
Cheers 88
child labor laws 31
choreographer 28, 31, 33
Clark, Susan 45–46
Cleveland, Davis 55, 108
clicker 141–142
Clooney, George 24
close-up 91, *92*, 97, 119–120, 125
Commedia dell'Arte 149
commercial breaks 119
composition of shots 91
Conn, Eileen 144
Contreras, Natalie 35
control booth 143
Coppage, Judy 10
The Cosby Show 15, 129
costume department 32; *see also* Replansky, Jessica
Coulier, Dave 79, 143
coverage 5, 14, 36, 48, 50, 98–99, *100*–102, *103*, 105, 107, *109*, 110, 113–116, *117*, 128, 140

169

Index

cowboy shot **92**, 97
craft 5–6, 9–10, 12, 27, 69, 78, 128, 131, 152, 157
cross the line 126
cross three-shot 47, 98, 104, 116
cross two-shot 47, 98, 100, 102, 111, 140
crosses 22, 42, 65, 71–73, **100**, 102, 106, 117, **118**, 124
crossing cameras **99**
cues 62–63, 65, 84, 138
Curry, Mark 136; see also Hangin' with Mr. Cooper

dance rehearsals 31, 85, 120
Dance with Me 155
Dancing with the Stars 142
Desilu studios 1
dialogue 6, 60–62, 64, 66, 71–74, 76, 90, 141, 146; see also dialogue coach
dialogue coach 37, 51, 90, 123–124; see also dialogue
directing from the booth 139–143, 145
directing on the floor 139–140, 143–145
director (first time) 17–19, 25–27, 41–42, 77
directorial vision 15, 67, 75, 126, 130, 133, 146–147, 152
director's cut 130, 133, 146
Director's Fellowship 19
Disney Channel 49, 85, 88–89
Dixon, Donna 1
Dog with a Blog 122
downstage 49, 74, 132
dry run 140

ECU (extreme close-up) 91–**92**, 97
entrances and exits 108–109
ER 18
Erving, Julius 136
establishing shot 117
Esther 155
ESU (electronic set-up) 7–8
Ewing, Patrick 136–137

executive producer 2, 9, 20, 33, 35, 38–40, 41–42, 61, 76, 89, 143–144, 154
eyes 48, 50–51, 97, 102, 104–105, 111, 114, 152

The Facts of Life 24
Family Matters 17, 60, 67, 136, 151–152
Family Ties 88
Fegan, Roshon 102
fight choreography 33
first team (principal actors) 120–121
"flanking" cameras 99
flat 50–50 two-shot 103
flat three-shot 116
flat two-shot 110
foreground cutting piece 50, 103
fourth wall 36, 104, 112
Fox, Michael J. 88
Foxx, Jamie 19–20
framing 5, 91, 103, 107, **109–110**, 114–115
Friends 15
full figure shot 92, 97
Full House 3, 17, 79, 85, 119, 135, 143, 150–152

Gangs of New York 130
Ganz, Lowell 24, 155
Garcia, Dina 69; see also Bailey, Ainsley
Geffen Theater 63
Girl Meets World 4
Glass, Ron 78
Godspell 149
Goldberg, Gary David 88
golden take 146
"good eyes" 97
Good Luck Charlie 25
Goodall, Daryn 35
Goulet, Robert 54
Grotowski, Jerzy 54, 149

Hackford, Taylor 63
Hagen, Uta 63
Hair 149
hand-held 18, 34
Hangin' with Mr. Cooper 136; see also Curry, Mark

Hanks, Tom 1–2, 20, 22–24, 56, 65, 126, 131, 157
Hansen, Scott 29
Happy Days 21, 23–24
Hardaway, Tim 136
HD cameras 107
Head of the Class 24
Hessenheffer, Tinka 102–103; see also Sunshine, Caroline
Hoffman, Bobby 23–24
"hooks" 1
Hopkins, Telma 1
Howard, Leo 132
Howard, Ron 21–22, 24

I Love Lucy 107, 133
insert shot **92**
inside coverage 101, 103, 105, 126, 133
Irigoyen, Adam 69, 102; see also Martinez, Deuce
It's a Living 2, 23

The Jamie Foxx Show 19
Jessie 4, 25, 138
jib 34–35
Johnson, Brandon 49; see also Wilde, Gary
Jones, CeCe 53, 58, 72, 80, 93, 106, 132, 144; see also Thorne, Bella
Jones, Georgia 53; see also Barone, Anita
Jones, Ty 102
Jordan, Michael 136

Karras, Alex 45–46
KC Undercover 4
Keaton, Buster 125
Keel, Howard 155
Kelada, Asaad 140
Kent State 65
Kern, Bob 126
Kickin' It 132
Kramer 58

La MaMa 1, 63, 149, 150, 154–155
Landers, David 21; see also Lenny and Squiggy
The Last Chance Saloon 154

Index

laugh spread 134
laugh track 139
Laverne & Shirley 1, 3, 11–12, 18, 21–24, 56, 61, 65, 70, 78, 126, 149; *see also* Marshall, Penny; Williams, Cindy
Lawrence, Carol 54
Lenny and Squiggy 21–22; *see also* Landers, David; Mckean, Michael
Lewis, Emmanuel 137; *see also* Webster
line-cut 140–143
line producer 31
line-reading 115
Linn-Baker, Mark 16, 39, 56–58
logline 13
long shot *92*
looking left to right 126
looking right to left 126
Lotterstein, Rob 20, 35, 54–55, 84, 86, 144

"Made in Japan" 86
La MaMa 1, 63, 149, 150, 154–155
Mandel, Babaloo 24
marked script 120, 140, 142
Marshall, Gary 12, 23, 108
Marshall, Penny 12, 21–22, 57, 70–72; *see also* Laverne & Shirley
Martinez, Deuce 69, 102; *see also* Irigoyen, Adam
The Mary Tyler Moore Show 12
master shot 50, 99, 101, 103, 105, 110–111, 114, 116–117, 119, 121, 123, 126, 141
matching two-shot 100, 110
Mckean, Michael 21; *see also* Lenny and Squiggy
medium shot 91–*92*
Meisner 63
Merry-Go-Round 155
Miller, Tom 23, 153; *see also* Miller-Boyett

Miller-Boyett 40, 88; *see also* Boyett, Bob; Miller, Tom
monitors 93, 142–143
Mork & Mindy 1, 3, 96; *see also* Williams, Robin
multi-camera 3–5, 15–17, 140
multiple prosceniums 105–106; *see also* proscenium
music cues 84
My Big Fat Greek Wedding 2, 4, 20

Nardino, Gary 23
network executive 9, 144
network run-through 7, 82–84, 87–88, 96, 98; *see also* producer run-through; run-through
The New Odd Couple 78

The Odd Couple 57, 78
O'Dell, Tony 90
"Off the Wall" 63
The Office 73
O'Horgan, Tom 149
Oklahoma! 10, 155
Olsen, Ashley 66, 79
Olsen, Mary-Kate 66, 79
on its feet 7, 42, 44, 47–48, 50–51, 61, 75, 77, 85
one against two shot 47, 102, 104
opening teaser 119
over-the-top 134

P.A. system 143
Pace, Frank 30, 154
Pair of Kings 123
Paramount (Studios) 1–2, 21, 23
pass coverage 113–115; *see also* second pass coverage
Payton, Gary 136
pedestal 34, 107
Perez, Phil 13–14, 124
Perfect Strangers 3, 16, 39, 56–57, 61
persona non grata 23
physical comedy 32, 39–40, 47, 53–60, 70–72, 120

pick-up shot 101, 114, 116, 123
pilot 1–2, 23, 38–40, 65, 88, 141, 150
Pinchot, Bronson 16, 39, 55–58, 72, 96
pink revised table draft 7, 32, 76, 82, 96; *see also* revisions
Pitt, Brad 24
Polish Lab Theater 54
politics 11, 27, 35, 41, 67, 123, 131, 152
post-production 33, 115, 122, 133, 139–140, 145–147
Potts, Annie 155
pre-shoot 7–8, 138
producer run-through 6–7, 65, 75, 77, 80, 82; *see also* network run-through; run-through
producer's medium 128
production meeting 6, 28–38, 41, 81
props 32, 44, 58, 72, 82–84, 87
proscenium 36, 73, 104–106, 111–112; *see also* multiple prosceniums

quad split 93–*94*, *99–100*, *102–103*, *109–110*, *114–115*, *117–118*
Queens College 65, 155

Rafkin, Alan 22
Raitt, John 155
Ray 63
Reiner, Carl 16
Reiner, Rob 16
Replansky, Jessica 32
resets 107–111; rolling reset *106*, 107; *see also* camera resets
residuals 150
re-staging 51, 145
return 111–112
revisions 8, 76–77; *see also* blue revised table draft; pink revised table draft
Rhoda 17

Index

Richman, Greg 35, 50
Rothman, Mark 155
run-through 55, 61, 69–70, 76–77, 85, 89, 130, 151; *see also* network run-through; producer run-through

Saget, Bob 79, 139, 143
Sandrich, Jay 141
"scenelets" 111
Schindler's List 25–26
Scolari, Peter 1, 126
Scorsese, Martin 130
script supervisor 62, 124, 145
The Second City 63
second pass coverage 114–115; *see also* pass coverage
second team 120; *see also* stand-ins
Seinfeld 15, 58
sequential order 135
set decorator 35
set designer 35
set plans 29
Shake It Up 3–4, 14, 17, 20, 26, 28, 34–35, 38, 43, 53, 56–57, 60, 66, 69, 80, 85, 106, 108, 129, 132, 134, 137, 144, 151
Shenandoah 155
shooting 5–8, 11–12, 14–17, 33–34, 36, 39, 44, 52, 69, 73, 78, 83, 85–86, 89–90, 92–100, 103–106, 108, 110, **112**–114, 116, 118, 120, 122–128, 133–135, 140–142, 144–145, 151, 156
shooting draft 7–8, 89–90, 98
shooting the joke 52
short wall 111, **112–113**
shot list 140
shots 2, 11, 34, 36, 51, 73, 79, 91–93, 97–99, 101, 103–104, 110, 115–116, 120–122, 125–126, 131, 134–135, 140–142, 144, 146–147, 157; *see also* camera shots; carry shot; close-up; composition of shots; cross three-shot; cross two-shot; establishing shot; flat 50–50 two-shot; flat three-shot; flat two-shot; full figure shot; insert shot; long shot; master shot; matching two-shot; medium shot; one against two shot; pick-up shot; single against two-shot; singles; specialty shots; super master shot; three-shot; T's shot; two-shot; two-shot against a single
"show and tell" 83
single against two-shot 102
single camera 5, 15, 18
singles 14, **16**, 93, 95, **99**, 102, 105, 114, 116, 121, 141
Slane, Stephan 155
slow-motion camera 34
Somers, Suzanne 21
sound effects 83–84
special effects 13, 28, 33, 82–84, 87
specialty shots 121–122
speed read-through 8, 138
Sperber, Wendi Jo 1
Spielberg, Steven 25–26
Splash 24
"square up the middle" 103
stage direction 36–37, 44, 77, 81
stage left 74, **108**, 114
stage manager 53, 142
stage notes 62
staging 5, 47–48, 51–52, 55, 59–60, 64, 69–71, 75–76, 90–91, 131, 153
Stamos, John 135–136
stand-ins 85, 120–121, 140; *see also* second team
standards and practices 88
Stanislavski's method 54
steadicam 34
Step by Step 67, 151
Stewart, Ellen 150
Strasberg, Lee 63
stunts 13, 33, 84
Sunshine, Caroline 102; *see also* Hessenheffer, Tinka
super master shot 116–117, **118**
sweetening 139
Sweetin, Jodie 66, 150
swing sets 35

table draft 47, 89
table read 6–7, 36–38, 41, 42, 52
tag 55
Taxi 1, 107, 141
Taylor, Holland 1, 80
The Ted Knight Show 156
30 Rock 73
Thompson, Chris 2, 56, 65
Thompson, John 136
Thompson, Tommy 129
Thorne, Bella 53, 66, 95; *see also* Jones, CeCe
three camera situation 106
three-shot 105, 116
three walls 104
Three's Company 21
title sequence 119
Tracy, John 142
Trexler, Chris 56
T's shot 91, **92**, 97, 121
Two and a Half Men 3, 73
"two eyes" 104
two-shot 14, 16, 47, 93, 95, **99**–100, 105, 110–111, 114, 116–119, 121, 126, 141
two-shot against a single 47, 101–102

UCLA College 152
upstage 50, 74
Urkel, Steve 17, 67, 136; *see also* White, Jaleel

video-tape 140
video village 93, 143
visual effect 33
visual quality 115

Wade, Dwyane 137
A Wake in Providence 4
wardrobe 30, 32, 87
warm-up person 139

Index

Warner Brothers 16, 88
Warren, Michael 39; Bickley-Warren 40
Webster 3, 45, 137, 141; *see also* Lewis, Emmanuel
weekly rundown 150
weekly schedule 7
Weinstein Brothers 130
Wheaton College 65
White, Jaleel 152; *see also* Urkel, Steve
Wilde, Gary 49; *see also* Johnson, Brandon
Williams, Cindy 11–12, 21–22, 57, 70; *see also Laverne & Shirley*
Williams, John 25
Williams, Robin 24, 63, 96; *see also Mork & Mindy*
Wilson, Demond 78–79
Winkler, Henry 21–22, 24
Witt-Thomas 23
wranglers 78, 80
writer's draft 28–29, 50

Yale School of Drama 65
Your Show of Shows 16

Zaharias, Babe 45
Zendaya 38, 48, 66, 95, 108; *see also* Blue, Rocky
Zwick, Hillary 150
Zwick, Jamie 150

www.ingramcontent.com/pod-product-compliance
Ingram Content Group UK Ltd.
Pitfield, Milton Keynes, MK11 3LW, UK
UKHW050523150426
5217IPUK00026B/1766